The Journeying Years
How they came to Auroville

Acknowledgements

The Journeying Years is published by PRISMA at Auroville.
© Dianna Bowler, 2009

Author : Dianna Bowler
Interviews : Dianna Bowler
Photographs : Nizam Merguei

Second Edition 2023

ISBN 978-93-95460-84-2 (Paperpack)
ISBN 978-93-95460-83-5 (ebook)

BISAC Code:
HIS062000, HISTORY / Asia / South / India
PHI034000, PHILOSOPHY / Social
JNF025000, JUVENILE NONFICTION / History / General

Thema Subject Category:
JBCC9, History of ideas
NH, History
NHF, Asian history
FC, Biographical fiction / autobiographical fiction

Cataloging-in-Publication Data for this title is available from the Library of Congress.

Published by:
PRISMA, an imprint of Digital Media Initiatives
PRISMA, Aurelec/ Prayogshala, Auroville 605101,
Tamil Nadu, India
www.prisma.haus

... the heart of the mystery of the journeying years ...

Auroville is a prayer and a curse,
A suspicious sidelong glance,
An explosion of silent love,
A temple in the sun
A fractured broken jar
A whisper in the wind
A laughter and a song
A strong fraternal clasp
A blasphemy of the Gods
A golden bodied truth
A prayer beyond the stars
A battlefield of bliss
A child against the sun
A bird against the sky
A golden thought unsung
A flame that is a cry
Towards an unknown earth
That in our hearts does rest
And slowly comes forth to birth
Breaking forth slowly.

Roger Harris.

CONTENTS

Introduction

Preface

Frederick ... who came from Germany in 1966 1

Kireet ... who came from Holland in 1971 6

Johnny ... who came from Australia in 1971. 11

Judith ... who came from England in 1972. 17

Bhaga ... who came from France in 1972 22

B ... who came from USA in 1974 27

Franz ... who came from Germany in 1974. 29

Gillian ... who came from Australia in 1977. 35

Joy ... who came from Pondicherry Ashram in 1977. 37

Tim ... who came from London in 1977. 40

Georges ... who came from Belgium in 1979 43

Auralee ... who came from Canada in 1981. 48

Sanjeev ... who came from Delhi in 1981. 53

Grace ... who came from Gandigram, Madurai, in 1987. 56

Banu ... who came from Villupuram, South India, in 1987. 61

Guy ... who came from Belgium in 1988 65

Mahalingam ... who came from South India in 1988. 69

Bob ... who came from England in 1988. 73

Holger ... who came from Germany in 1990. 78

Ashok ... who came from North India in 1990 83

Vladimir ... who came from the Ukraine in 1992. 86

Christine ... who came from Germany in 1995. 90

Kalsang ... who came from Dharamsala in 1995.. 92

Shankar ... who came from Kuilapalayam village near Auroville in 1995 95

Ricardo ... who came from Argentina in 1997. 99

Martin ... who came from Switzerland in 1997 103

Deep ... who came in 1998 from Calcutta 108

Sarasija ... who came from South Korea in 1999.. 110

Shailaja ... who came from Baroda, North India, in 2001 114

Valeria ... who came from Italy in 2002.. 119

Aviram and Yorit ... who came from Israel in 2002 125

Audrey ... who came from the USA in 2003. 130

Lavkamad ... who came from Agra, India, in 2004 133

Dianna ... who came from England in 2005. 137

Manohar ... who came from Italy in 2005 141

A Young Tamil man ... who came from Pondicherry 146

INTRODUCTION

Auroville is an international community on the eastern side of South India, 160 kilometres south of Chennai (previously Madras). Auroville has been established since 1968, and in the year 2008 proudly celebrated its 40th anniversary. The fact that it still exists in this difficult South Indian environment is remarkable, and it is now world famous as an experiment in a spiritual and innovative way of living.

It was created by the Mother – who lived in the nearby Pondicherry Ashram – in 1968. She named it Auroville, "The City of Dawn," a city where a new consciousness could facilitate a new way of living that would be available to people from all over the world. She chose this dry and dusty plateau near the Bay of Bengal as a suitable site for Auroville, pointed on the map to where a huge banyan tree already existed, and selected the tree as the geographical centre of the future city. Mother herself never visited the place, as she was then 92 and too frail for the rough ride out from the Ashram in Pondicherry. Today, some 40 years later, the golden globe of Matrimandir is finally completed, and stands proudly by the banyan tree as "the soul of Auroville."

The Mother was born in 1878 into an educated Parisian family of bankers. Her mother was Egyptian and father Turkish and she was named Mirra Alfassa. As a girl she had many occult experiences which she later developed by studying in Algeria with Max Theon. She also lived in Japan for four years. In 1914 she came to Pondicherry, and upon meeting Sri Aurobindo immediately recognised him as the dark skinned man in a white dhoti who had visited her in dreams for many years.

Sri Aurobindo was born in 1872 in Calcutta and was sent at the age of seven with his two brothers to study in England. His father had high ambitions for his three sons, which at that time meant joining the Indian Civil Service that was "only accessible to the natives" after an English education. The boys did not return home for 13 years. On his return Sri Aurobindo could not speak to his family in their native tongue as he did not know Bengali, though he was an excellent scholar in Latin and Greek. He became passionately involved in the "Quit India movement," and at one time became "the most wanted man in India" by the British authorities. During a long period of imprisonment he had many deep spiritual experiences, and on his release received an inner directive to go to Pondicherry.

Pondicherry at that time was a French protectorate, and even today is a beautiful town with French colonial houses and Catholic churches. The Ashram developed around Sri Aurobindo, as is the Indian tradition, and when The Mother joined him in 1920 it eventually became a self-supporting community with workshops, library, and an excellent school. It now occupies a large part of the old town and is a centre of pilgrimage for thousand of Indians who recognize Sri Aurobindo as their guru and the greatest yogi-philosopher of the 20th century.

In the early 1970s the Sri Aurobindo Society, encouraged by the support of the Indian government and the recognition of UNESCO in 1966, worked to establish the foundations of Auroville. In time, differences of opinion inevitably developed and the two became separate entities. Today, however, there is a lively exchange between the two, the Ashram – broadly speaking – being the centre where one can develop one's own inner consciousness in a disciplined environment, and Auroville being an outward expression of that consciousness being lived in community.

The Mother gave very specific guidelines for the development of Auroville, which after 40 years of constant growth and change the Aurovilians are still aspiring to realise. Mother's vision was always magnificent, far reaching and profound. Thousands of visitors from all over the world come to see Auroville, and some stay on and decide to make it their home.

For some people this can be a long and difficult decision; for others it has been simple and direct.

Here are some of their stories. I hope you find them interesting, and even inspirational.

PREFACE

I first came here thirty five years ago on an afternoon's bicycle ride from Pondicherry, at that time a sleepy little French Indian town. To me, fresh from England's green and pleasant land, Auroville looked like the end of the world. The earth was red and scorched by the sun, devastated by flocks of hungry goats, and the local villages were poverty stricken. A few hundred hippy-looking westerners were cycling around or digging a huge hole under a banyan tree "to put the Matrimandir into," as I was told in broken English by a sun-crazed-looking French man. "The what?" I thought.

When I came back thirty years later I saw a miracle had taken place. Two million trees had been planted, eleven farms and eight schools had been developed, and the Matrimandir was a magnificent, golden globe. People lived in a variety of interesting houses in communities with magic names such as "Adventure", "Grace", "Courage." Something was definitely going on here!

Since the population was still only 2,000 people - the same as a small village or maybe five London streets - I realized there must be a very special quality in the people who lived here to have created such a vast change in such a short time. I wondered what had motivated them to leave their comfortable lives and come to live in Auroville. I was curious how they had first heard of this remote place, and then by what circuitous routes, both physical and spiritual, they had arrived here. Had they been immediately attracted and stayed on permanently, or did they come and go over the years? What sort of work did they do, and did they have any choice in the matter? How did they support themselves, or were they taken care of by the community? I became fascinated by this experiment in an utterly different way of live.

When I started asking people how they came to Auroville the answers were very varied, and often quite moving. Some of the older people had actually met the Mother, who passed away in 1973, and had received such a powerful experience from her that they were moved to change their lives completely. Many came to stay in the Pondicherry Ashram for a period, and then moved out to Auroville. They were inspired by the founding of The City of Dawn in 1968, and wanted to be involved in its future.

I thought it might be interesting and even helpful for others on the path - and indeed we are all on some sort of path - to write down some of the stories of how people came to Auroville. This compilation is the result.

Dianna Bowler

... A long beginning only has been made ...

FREDERICK ... WHO CAME FROM GERMANY IN 1966

I feel Germany has always had a cultural affinity with India through poets like Schopenhauer and Goethe. My mother was always searching for answers to life, and great Indian thinkers like Rabindranath Tagore and Ramakrishna meant a lot to her. A yoga teacher used to come to our house and teach us asanas. As a young kid when the American troops marched into Germany I had seen the U.S. G.I.s, and especially the black G.I.s with their pockets full of chocolate and chewing gum and they seemed like super men to me, and I thought America must be God's special place and the Americans his special people. Just after my high school, when I was about nineteen years old, I remember I wanted to go to America. I couldn't go to America as I had visited East Berlin, a communist country. As it was during McCarthy's time I was barred from entering America. So I decided that instead of going West I would go East.

For years I had questioned why the Nazis and Hitler had come to power in such a cultured country as Germany, and felt it as an insoluble tension and a burden in my life. I wanted to find answers for these questions as I had always felt like an exile in Germany.

I thought India may have some answers, so I set sail, and in December 1959 my boat landed in Bombay. India was very different in those days, poor and strange with few foreigners, but I will never forget my first response to India. I immediately felt at home, as if a tension that had always been there had been lifted. Gandhi and Tagore with their policy of non-violence and a spiritual attitude to life were role models for my generation, and so I felt a great affinity for this strange country. I travelled around and stayed for a few happy months at Tagore's Shantiniketan as a part-time student. I had read Sri Aurobindo in a German translation called "Indian Contribution to the Modern World", which included Vivekananda, Gandhi, Ramana Maharshi and Sri Aurobindo. As Sri Aurobindo had lived in Pondicherry, I thought I would come down and see his Ashram, though I wanted him "pure" and was rather suspicious about the French lady, called the Mother.

I stayed at the Castellini guest house and went to Mother's early morning Darshans, which didn't make much impression on me, so I thought as a matter of courtesy I should have an individual interview with her. That Darshan changed my life.

I opened the door to her room and at first I couldn't see her, as her chair was right behind the door, but she called me and I turned around. I knelt down in front of her. Being a young and arrogant student of philosophy I had

Frederick

prepared a good question for her, something like, "If everything in life becomes one, how can love be possible? Don't you need two poles for love to be manifest?" but I never got around to asking her. She asked me if I would like to speak or be silent, but I just couldn't speak. Her eyes went on a trip inside me – I went with her into myself. It was as if every little corner was lit up, as if I was totally known, not approved of or criticized, just looked at. It was such liberation, such an experience. Then she showed me something like one of those clear glass test tubes that rose above my head to infinity, a kind of column which lit up and at the bottom was a beautiful blue liquid. It was shown to me that that liquid is what you are now and that empty lit-up column is what you can become if you fulfil your destiny. She was very loving, and gave me a flower as I knelt there with my head on her knees. I came out of her room on wings, and for hours walked on the beach in a state of complete happiness.

I saw her many times after that – on my birthday, at Darshan or pujas or inaugurations. I wrote to her and told her I was going to serve her, give my life to her. Then something else happened. Mother's friend from Japan, Mrs Koybayashi, had been to visit her, and I thought I would like to go to Japan. I went by boat with the first batch of young people who were travelling on the land-route to Australia via Timor and then by postal boat across to Darwin. It was a very mixed-up year for me. I finally got to Japan, and somehow within a few days found myself enrolling in a Zen monastery; had my head shaved; wore a kimono; and was given lots of disciplines to follow. I completely forgot about Mother and became fascinated with Buddhism.

In March 1961 I came back to the Ashram, and went to Mother's Darshan with a very strong and critical mind, but when I met her I again had nothing to say. In despair I went back to Germany to study. I think these were the hardest days of my life. I felt I had no interior life but just the hard shell of a rich, spoilt young man. One evening I remember going to the opening of an art show in Brussels and I walked through the large gallery alone. There were paintings of Mother and Sri Aurobindo and I stood for a long while looking at a picture of the Mother. Then I knew;"My time has come to go back to the Ashram." I felt absolutely clear about this, yet I told my professor I was taking my thesis for my M.A. with me and I would be back soon. I sold my car and rented out my house, so obviously I had no intention of ever coming back.

In 1966 I came to India for good. I came to the Ashram Samadhi and laid my head on the grey cement block, as it was then, and made a promise to Mother that here I was surrendering my life to her like a monk. I felt very sorry for myself, but believed this sacrifice had to be made. When I lifted my head, I saw standing opposite me a beautiful blonde Swedish girl and I immediately fell in love with her. She had three children from her previous marriage, but we became very close, and after a while wanted to live together. Mother permitted us to do this, though it caused a scandal in the Ashram.

I had given whatever I had to the Mother. She told me she accepted it, but I was to be the trustee for it, so I used to give her monthly accounts of the money. Auroville was preparing for its inauguration, and my Swedish friend and I were excited by the idea of the City of Dawn, and used to go and visit the area and walk over the bare red earth. Eventually we decided we wanted to be part of it, and built a hut in what is now called Certitude. Our first son was born in Promesse and Mother arranged a doctor for us and he was entered into a big book as the first Auroville child.

We later had a meeting with Mother to decide where we should build a more suitable house. She said it should be in a central place and decided on

Certitude." You must build a proper house to show to the world that you are here for good," she told us. It was quite a three year sadhana building that house, as then there were no roads or electricity and water had to be brought in barrels. Piero was the architect, and he learned many of his skills as an engineer for building the Matrimandir from his work on our house.

That is how I came to Auroville.

Taking with Frederick after 43 years.

I have now been here 42 years; a long time, nearly half a lifetime. Auroville has always given me the opportunity to express myself in physical work, which has been the total opposite of what I was brought up to do, as I studied philosophy and language, which are totally abstract. In my first few years here I found myself responsible for a family of six living in a barren desert in a backward rural area with no water, shelter or roads. I had to get it together to provide a house for the family, then some sort of schooling for the children. We built the first pucca house in Auroville at Certitude, which is still occupied by our family. I always regret my lack of physical skills as I have had to work for 40 years as a dilettante. I have big hands but no technical expertise. Nevertheless, I have built a lot of houses and dug a lot of wells and very much enjoyed the experience.

I always saw Auroville as intended by Mother for collective endeavours. She said that the next stage of consciousness will be received by collective receptacles – it is too large for an individual. In my own experience, whenever I have felt "that special Auroville experience" it has always been as part of a team or group, whether it was in meditation or work or games. Again, from my own experience, whenever I have become isolated I notice I can go off at a tangent and become narrow and insular. Sports have been my saviour in this respect, bringing me together with others, especially the Tamil boys. It has provided a focus for my energy and competitiveness which has been good, for me - and for everyone else.

I was fortunate that I came from a well-to-do family, and when I met Mother I offered her all my money. She accepted it graciously and told me she would keep it for me. I must admit that in the years after her death I often woke up at 2 a.m. in a cold sweat of insecurity and regret, but I now realize that if I had kept a nest-egg it would have severely limited me. I know I have an arrogant streak in me, and on the occasions when I had to approach committees "cap in hand" and ask for help it was always uncomfortable, but somehow I could always do it. I always felt I was part monk, part playboy, and Mother obviously recognized this and communicated with me on those levels. Mother was never prudish; she was often jokey with me and used to laugh at my conflicts.

Sri Aurobindo and Mother never turned away from money in the traditional Indian way, but had the courage to include it in their integral yoga. I always remember a talk Mother had with an American student: "I want you to go to America and raise money," she told him. Two months later he had not gone. When she addressed him again he said, "Let me live a simple and humble life, I don't want to get involved with money." Mother replied: "I saw a million dollars waiting for you there!" I bet he felt really bad.

My children are now grown up and all living in Auroville, which says something very positive about this place. Often in the early days we parents worried about the lack of educational facilities, and experimented ourselves in many wild and wonderful ways. We tried many varieties of schooling, including boarding away from here, and often felt worried at what we might be putting our children through. But when I look at them now, with their confidence and naturalness, I feel proud of them. When I look back at my childhood after the second World War and how fear and insecurity were imbibed into me, I feel good for my children when I see their openness. When you ask them the traditional question, "What do you want to be?" they answer something like, "Happy." That would have been considered scandalous in my childhood.

Maybe it is sad that Auroville today lacks the adventures of previous years. I don't know. For me it was a fantastic adventure playground.

Mother on sports

We do not want to reject the body, but transform it. For this, physical education is one of the means most directly effective.

We want to come in contact with the supreme consciousness, the universal consciousness; we want to bring it down in ourselves and to manifest it. But for that we must have a very solid base; our base is our physical being in our body. Therefore we have to build up a body solid, healthy, enduring, skilful, agile and strong, ready for everything. We are here for special work – a work that cannot be done elsewhere. For that we must have a very solid base – our base is our physical body. There is no better way to prepare the body than physical exercise; sports, athletics, gymnastics, and all the games are the best means to develop and strengthen the body.

KIREET ... WHO CAME FROM HOLLAND IN 1971

As a young child my greatest dream was to travel around the world, and when I was twelve I made a pact with my friend that we would do this trip together. When we were twenty one the time had come, and we set off for the long, overland journey to Kabul, by car. Meanwhile war had broken out in Pakistan, so we only could go as far as Tehran, and had to stay there for a while. I got a job as a salesman and managed to save some money, and when the danger had passed we drove on to Pakistan. There I got seriously ill, and had to spend all my money on hospitals and medicines. While I was lying there for weeks, I began to realize that what I really wanted to do was to go to India and study yoga. The Paks told me it was a dirty, dreadful country and that I was crazy to even think about it, but when I got well I made my way down to Bangalore. I had been interested in yoga for many years and had been very impressed by Ruud Lohman's book on yoga, "Alle dingi nieuw". I had also dipped into Sri Aurobindo but had not understood very much.

As Ruud was in Auroville I decided to visit the place. I took a rickshaw from town then walked up the gentle slope towards where Hope community now is ... and suddenly I felt very happy ... a sort of feeling of lightness and freedom. As I passed a man on the dusty road he called out to me, "You look very happy." We started talking and I asked him where I could find Ruud and he replied, "At the bottom of a very big hole." When I finally found Ruud I discovered he was working on the foundations of the Matrimandir, carrying buckets of cement with western and Tamil workers under the scorching sun. Ruud invited me to stay with him in Peace, later called the Camp, and I helped with the concreting. To me it all felt like a big party; "Yoga with the wheelbarrow."

I loved Auroville, and stayed here for a few months working in the nursery, but my friend wanted to continue our world trip, and as I felt committed to him,

I had to leave Auroville. But the vision of that wonderful space and freedom I had experienced stayed with me.

I returned in 1972 and went to the Ashram to see the Mother for a personal interview. In those days she chose you by looking at your photograph, and she must have seen my great need because she chose me. She told me to take off my glasses, and I remember her piercing eyes looking right into my soul. When I came out of her room I burst into tears. I realized something very profound had happened to me, and my life would never be the same again.

My wife came back with me to Auroville in 1975, but everything had changed greatly. The quarrel with the Ashram had begun and work on the Matrimandir had come to a halt. I stayed in Utility, which at that time seemed to be the most organized community and did strenuous yoga taught by Nergez. I remember being fascinated by the canyons which at that time were red and deep and carried off huge amounts of the precious rain water. This led to the soil erosion that had made Auroville a barren desert.

My wife, however, was not happy living here, either in Auroville or in India, so we decided to return to Holland and help Auroville in any way we could. We raised money for a Tamil children's school by holding concerts, slide shows, and running lotteries. We still receive money from many of these Dutch people, which is really nice. We divorced in 1995, so my hope of returning to Auroville with money to build a school and a house for our family was completely dashed. I was devastated.

All was not lost, however, as my mother loved India and wanted to come and live in Auroville with me. She gave me the money to build a house, and together we established Gaia's Garden as a beautiful guest house. So my dream did become true, in a very roundabout way, as dreams often do. I felt completely at home.

Talking to Kireet after 37 years

I came to stay on 21st May 1972, but I still feel like a Newcomer in the spirituality. The integral yoga demands a lot, and I often feel that I can't even fulfil the basic requirements. That is the reason I am here in Auroville, and I often feel I need a bang on the head to make me remember that. I get so busy and occupied with my world that I forget the Divine. My meeting with the Mother all those years ago had such a tremendous impact on my life that I still have a very strong connection with her, and that is still carrying me through.

1972 here in Auroville was a golden time. By 1976 everything had changed and I found it very uncomfortable, so I stayed in Pondicherry and used to travel in every day. I later stayed in Utility and used to walk down the canyons, and I remember thinking that there should be some dams here as the erosion was vey serious. Years later that is what I worked on, and that is where I finally built my house – all very strange.

I worked in Matrimandir Gardens and then in Shakti, where Walter taught me about the indigenous plants. We used to go out and collect seeds from the temple groves, and I remember loving it, but coming back covered in scratches that took ages to heal. In the evenings I used to supervise the building of my house, so that was a very busy time. I always believed that if you want to teach the Tamil people you have to work with them, and show them the standards you want. We always had a nice relationship and I got to know their families and their difficulties. I never did manage to learn much of the Tamil language however; it always sounds to me like a soup or as if it is all glued together.

When I went to visit the local Bommaiyapalayam village school I was horrified. I had been a teacher in Holland for 23 years, and could not understand the neglect and ignorance I saw here. I was able to get some Dutch people to give donations and sponsor children, and created a good school. It is still going strong, though I am not actively involved in it now.

Kireet

When I used to walk with my dog in the canyon I saw how the topsoil was regularly washed away in the monsoon, and the sea turned blood red as it washed into the Bay of Bengal. I strongly felt we should put in check dams to conserve the precious water, so I started checking the existing ones. I couldn't believe what I saw. The builders had cheated on the materials and used inferior concrete, so all the dams were broken. The holes looked like Emmenthal cheese, and in some places it was possible to harvest honey from the bee's nests in the concrete. I got a good team of men together and showed them how to build the dams, but all the time checking them and their work. I used to work with the men to educate and encourage them, carrying granite which eventually gave me awful back pain. The Apollo hospital in Chennai told me a disc had broken and I might end up in a wheelchair, very awkward for getting up and down the canyon. I have learned to control the pain, though my days of lifting granite are now over.

Meanwhile my mother, who was living in Holland, decided she wanted to come and live with me in Gaia's Garden, which was the name of a similar place I had built up in Holland. We both underestimated the effect of the tropical weather on an older fragile person however, and she got tropical amoebas that weakened her. I thought she was developing Altzheimer's disease as she was becoming vague and irritable, and I didn't have any idea how to look after her. We decided it would be best for her to return to Holland, and now she is well cared for in a Residential Home and is bright and well again.

I was 46 when I came to Auroville, and didn't want to be dependant on a maintenance, so I decided that running a guest house would be a good way of financing myself while also providing a service for Auroville. I wanted to do it well, as this was the second time I was establishing a house and way of life; I couldn't bear the thought of there ever being a third time. Now the guest house and the large garden are established, I really enjoy running it. I feel I am an ambassador for Auroville and try to give good service to the guests. I get all sorts of people staying here, and many come back again and again. Some are very interesting and we often have great conversations. Quite a few have even become Newcomers, so I am pleased about that. I have posters up telling the guests about the village school and the work with the dams, and often I take them on visits, which they love.

Seven years ago I got married to Younge, a beautiful Korean woman. Although most couples here do not get married, after much thought we decided to for various reasons, apart from the romantic ones. If ever we did have to leave India it might be very difficult for Younge to enter Holland as a Korean, but as an official couple it would be much easier. Also, her parents are quite conservative, and must have been worried about this foreigner their daughter was marrying, so we felt it was a responsibility to them. We married in Korea and it was a glorious occasion.

So that is my life now. It is as if all the pieces of a puzzle have come together, and I am very satisfied and happy with it.

JOHNNY ... WHO CAME FROM AUSTRALIA IN 1971

I had my first sense of India lying in bed as a little boy in a Sydney suburb staring at a carving of an ebony elephant with ivory tusks; it used to fascinate me. Then at school I remember a teacher reading to us from "The Diaries of Marco Polo", and I was transfixed by the exotic and fabulous adventures. We had this custom at High School of former students coming to talk to us about their careers, usually boring ones like accountants or managers, but once we had these two big, hairy adventurous guys who I think had been missionaries in Africa. I was very inspired by them, as I imagined them saving the natives from pythons in the jungle. All these impressions were stored away in my head, like compost for my future.

As a boy I remember poring over copies of "Popular Mechanics" when the family was asleep, and making a crystal set with military headphones. I was always a crackpot kid, taking motor bikes apart, and for months my father let me use the garage for all my stuff and parked his car in the driveway. The biggest days of my life were when people cleared out their attics and garages and dumped all the stuff on the front pavement. I would sneak days off school and go around and collect it and bring it home.

Sydney in the early 1960's was a very conservative and Americanised place. Certain influences from the outside world were beginning to creep in, and I was greedy for them. I was alert enough at 16 to read an anthology that was required reading for all hippies; "Mornings of Magic" I think it was called. Rudolph Steiner, Wilhem Reich and Sri Aurobindo were included in the book, and my eyes began to open. I was earning money at the age of 14, and on Saturday nights I would go with my friend who was part Aboriginal into the city for a Chinese meal. That's as daring as it got in those days. Then things opened up in Sydney with a little cinema called the Savoy that showed New Wave French films – Jean Luc Goddard, Bergman, Truffaut – which showed me a whole new world of sophistication. This place was fascinating to me, as I met interesting people sitting on cushions on the floor – I'd never seen that before – burning joss sticks under a big picture of Madame Blavatsky. It inspired a generation looking for something different from the beer drinking, free living society we had created. We made our own hippy flowing clothes and started festivals and welcomed flower power with open arms.

Through all this period I somehow kept up my architectural studies for five years, but dropped out before finishing the sixth year, much to my parent's despair. They had always been loving and supportive of me, but found this rejection difficult to take. My father was a judge, and my mother came from a family of doctors, so their backgrounds were conventional and it was too much for them. Especially as that year I got married, had a baby, and got a job as a taxi driver.

My life changed abruptly when Buckminster Fuller, the progressive, far-out architect, came to my college to give a lecture. He had tremendous energy and concentration and was the first radical thinker I had met. He was felt to be a threat to conventional architecture and engineering, and in a subtle way I think he demolished many ideas in modern architecture. He was my hero. I wanted to be just like him.

My son Jonas, who is now 41, suffered badly as a young child from severe food allergies, which were very stressful for us all. My wife Jan decided to take him to the Pondicherry Ashram to try and find a cure for him. Jonas was only three at the time, and the only white child in the Ashram school, but within a few months on their diet of rice, curd and bananas he became a strong healthy child; it was like a miracle.

I went to work in the mines in Cairns in northern Australia to make money to come to Auroville. My wife had written to me that Auroville was a wonderful place; "A place of tribal music on a hill overlooking the sea" was how she tried to lure me there. In 1971 there were about 150 people in Auroville and it was administered by the Society. Mother was still alive then, and used to advise us, as we were often in very difficult and confusing situations. At that time Aspiration was the largest community and full of French spiritual snobs. I remember they all shaved their hair off at the same time as if they were part of a cult. When I went to the sort of entry group they had and told them I was an architect, they were very pleased and suggested I could work with Frenchman Roger Anger. I refused point blank, as I hadn't come all this way just to continue the same work that my heart wasn't in. I was told there was no place for me in Auroville then, so I went to live on the beach near Quiet with my wife.

I used my years of architectural training and my memories form Popular Mechanics to start building small keet houses. We could build a simple house with four granite pillars, a platform and a veranda in three days using four men. We later developed the capsule style and there was a huge demand for them. I found a soul-mate in Ramu, a Tamil man in whom I sort of saw myself mirrored in a different culture, and we used to speak a geometrical, not linear, similar language.

It was the perfect life, working up in Auroville in the day and going back to the Quiet beach at night. It felt good to offload some of that information I had been stuffing my head with for five years, and I was free to make mistakes, as we were only working in bamboo and keet, not concrete. The plan was to start a small settlement, plant trees and establish a night watchman, and then move on to repeat the procedure. Mother always said the forest should have few people living there, and she herself called our place "Fertile."

Our house at Quiet eventually got caught up in a dispute, and we even took it to court, then got tired of fighting and decided to leave. The Pondicherry admission committee refused us admission for Auroville, so we went to ask Mother what we should do. "What's the problem? Don't worry about it" she said, and we realized this was an unofficial way of getting in. The Fertile community asked us to come and live with them, and we were very happy to take up their offer We always felt we had Mother's support, love and encouragement, and she gave us the very first plant for our garden.

Talking to Johnny after 36 years

I have now been here for 36 years, and been through many stages. The first one was teaching the fishermen how to fish. A friend of mine who had a degree in fishing joined me in making a catamaran, and we showed them how to do it, which of course was a total disaster. We then moved up the hill, and with a third generation farmer from Alsace showed the farmers how to farm. The arrogance! We then learned to watch the Tamils and do what they had been doing for thousands of years.

In 1972 we went to live in Fertile, and started re-forestation. At that time there were no trees, just an odd one here or there. I remember the fisher women running across the burning sand with baskets of fish on their heads to get shelter under the next tree, maybe a kilometre away. Our main priority was to get shade. We organized a bullock cart to continuously bring us up water from the village, and began to plant trees. We had no idea what we were planting, and just grew whatever the government scheme gave us. The villagers thought we were crazy planting trees that didn't give fruit or were not for firewood. As soon as a sapling was big enough they would come and cut it down for firewood. I got in many fights over that. They would bring their hungry goats up to eat our grass; our damming of the water stopped it flowing into their ponds ... they felt very threatened by us stupid new colonialists.

The land at that time was an arid desert due to generations of overgrazing, but they had worked out a system for survival with it. The rains were very dependable in those days, and after the first rains they would bring up bullock loads of compost and plough the land. On the second rains they would sow the seeds, and three months later they would come and harvest the ragi, black gram, peanuts and millet. It was reckoned that a villager needed two acres to feed his family and as many kids as possible to help him in the field. This pattern continued till the 1980's, when India had an 18 million dollar World Bank Debt and Indira Gandhi started making changes. The government gave subsidies and encouraged the planting of cash crops, which in this area were cashews. A farmer could make 5,000 rupees growing millet or he could make 20,000 growing cashews; there was no choice. This changed everything, as the farmers were no longer self-sufficient but became cash croppers. They had fewer children and created the "South Indian miracle" in one generation, by reducing the size of their families from seven kids to three. These kids became educated, and are now the new consumers. Every time I go to Pondicherry I see a new sort of bicycle – Chinese or South Korean in endless varieties and colours.

I originally thought schooling was unnecessary, but eventually the kids said; "Johnny, we need a school." They made their own desks in crazy shapes and we set up the Fertile School, which later joined Last School. The old school is now being resurrected as an art school where anyone can come and have the space to do funky things like sculpture, engraving, woodblock printing. I feel creative art now has a low profile in Auroville, and this building could provide a space for it. I love working with kids, especially at crazy theatrical projects, but my annual favourite is the Christmas Fair at the Youth Centre which Paul and I have done for 12 years now. I have acquired a weird collection of fairground games, such as giant punch bags and skittles, and am now making an adventure climbing frame for a school in Thiruvanamalai.

A group of us set up the Youth Centre, but it has always been a controversial place in many ways. It is in the wrong situation, and now the ring road will go through it. The kids built the place for themselves, and recently re-roofed the

Johnny

kitchen and built a workshop. I think it is a living art school and there are some good artists there. You can see the difference compared with Kailash, the other place which was built for the kids to live in, which they don't particularly feel involved with.

My main claim to fame, I believe, is the creation of the "capsule". It is now even on the internet! It started with the invention of the portable toilet, which was filled within a few months, then had a tree planted on it, and the toilet moved to another spot. The women were complaining about lack of privacy, so I developed a simple crystaline, octohydren shape based on the triangle that could be moved around. Thus began the ubiquitous Auroville house. People came up to me and said, "I'd like one too", so we began building them. They were like a self-contained portable space capsule; I guess nowadays they are called "pods". I have made them in England, Moscow and Japan, and a few of the original ones still exist in Auroville. Tata, the Indian industrialist, came here years ago to have a look at Auroville and told Frederick; "The single best thing Auroville has done is develop the capsule."

Now I am still living here in Fertile where I landed 36 years ago. It is still a sort of "Old McDonald's Farm" with chickens and cows and half a dozen people living here. Of course Auroville has changed an awful lot and there are lots of big houses, but I believe we need all flavours, all variations for our city, and for an expression of Human Unity we need more than only white mid-Europeans. A Bombay film crew were here last year, and after looking around the place asked me, quite seriously, "Do you promote discomfort here?" I answered them something like; "Well, I grow my own vegetables, milk my own cows, and educate my own children. I think that's a very comfortable way to live." I don't know what they thought.

I came here 36 years ago and somehow I stayed on. I have never looked back. I think it is all a matter of surrender, of realizing a situation, then just following your nose.

JUDITH ... WHO CAME FROM ENGLAND IN 1972

When I look back at how my life has gone I can see how much came from my father, who was a Congregational vicar in the north of England. They are the free-minded, pioneering, anti-hierarchical branch of British Christianity. I think those forces have fuelled my life from my hippy days in London in the sixties, to my travelling overland to India by bus and then my 36 years here in Auroville. I remember a lady missionary coming to our children's Sunday school and telling us about South India, where people sat on the floor and ate off banana leaves and never had baths, always showers. I was fascinated, and wanted to be a lady missionary also.

I wanted to be adventurous, yet I felt cowardly. I wanted to be a hippy, yet I always felt a fraud, not quite the genuine article. I tried to hitch-hike to London once but never got a lift and came home. I finally did get to London on the train, and stayed with my sister Shraddhavan. My sensible bourgeois world was turned upside down by London life; I was challenged to the roots. I got a job as a maid which I really liked, but nobody thought it was a proper job, so I got a job as a teacher, but hated it. I'd gone from school as a pupil to a school as a teacher, which was awful, so I quit after a short time. I felt absolutely confused by my life, but somehow realised something had to be done, so I started saving money for travelling.

My life changed forever when I met a middle aged eccentric German man called Jost in The World's End pub in Chelsea, London. He had been to the Sri Aurobindo Ashram in Pondicherry, so we asked him to come to our London flat and tell us about it. I wasn't particularly impressed with him, but when he started to tell us about the Mother and Sri Aurobindo I was fascinated, and I knew I must go to Pondicherry.

I found a bus that was going overland to India, and went and got my £40 ticket, one way of course, from a hole-in-the-wall ticket office. (How I trusted people in those days!) I had given away everything I owned, and bought a canvas horse-nose bag to carry my few clothes and a picture of Mother and Sri Aurobindo. A smart looking bus picked me up, with a bunch of very hippy-looking young people, and friends waved me off. The bus got as far as Croydon, about 20 miles away, then we all had to get out and change to what I can only describe, though I didn't know it then, as an Indian village bus with bars on the windows and hard seats. The owner-driver was an enterprising Anglo-Indian who was driving his English wife and two children to Delhi, a trip that was advertised as taking about one month.

I remember the journey as a series of snapshots; the German super motorways of which I had never seen the like, and the memory of being hungry all through Germany. When we stopped to eat at the motorway cafés they only had food from machines and we had no German coins. We slept on the beaches in Greece, which I found terribly exciting, but discovered how macho the men were as we moved away from the safety of England. In Istanbul I was introduced to crazy, terrifying driving, though in those days there was very little traffic, but I was still horrified. I loved Istanbul with its mosques and minarets, but my main memory is of a man carrying a grand piano on his back up a long slope. Turkey seemed very bare and rough as we left the greenery of Europe behind. I wore, for the whole journey, a sort of kaftan I had made from an Indian bedspread I had bought in Portobello market that covered me from head to toe. Several Turkish men told me how they appreciated my covering up, as most of the girls were still in shorts and skimpy little nothings and caused a scandal wherever they went. U.S. Nato missiles seemed to be everywhere in Turkey, and very scary. After all, this was 1971 and the Turkish border adjoined the Soviet Union. As we drove to the Iranian border our driver warned us, "Make sure everything is 100% clean in the bus as they have the death penalty here"; that sobered us a little. Teheran seemed to be a very modern city after all those primitive villages we had driven through, but we were glad to leave as things felt pretty hostile, especially towards the women in our group.

Afghanistan was unbelievably stark and high and cold with mountain upon mountain range stretching into the distance. I remember our group trooping into a tea shop and sitting on the floor and being surrounded by these dignified, strong looking men in magnificent robes smoking their hookahs and completely ignoring us. We looked horribly dirty and dishevelled compared to their rocklike dignity, and I felt very inferior. Although they had a refinement I also felt they were probably lacking in all compassion. The women of course were head to toe in heavy black with only a little grill over their face; I was fascinated. This was years before the Russian invasion but Kabul already looked ruinous and wrecked. I will never forget my night high up in the Khyber Pass. We got a puncture right at the highest point, so had to make camp and spend the night there, which was highly dangerous and illegal. The moon was full and the mountains magnificent, then a silent group of Pathans encircled us with their rifles (these were the days before Kalashnikovs), and sat there, without talking, till the dawn. I suppose they were protecting us – I'll never know.

We drove down into Pakistan in the middle of the night, down into the heat, and the border army put us in a swamp full of mosquitoes till morning. Rawalpindi and Peshawar were dusty and dirty, and I remember a group of young men amusing themselves by pushing over a young boy with only one leg. Not a country I would like to go back to again. India began with the brown muddy waters of what I supposed was the Indus river, and two vultures sitting on a dead cow pecking its eyes out. I was amazed at all the bicycles and thousands of young men everywhere. I sat there and thought; "What on earth am I doing here? Why have I chosen this crazy place?" I didn't know why, so just kept going. Things picked up as we drove into Delhi, as I was amazed at the beautiful city Lutyens had designed. It seemed so civilised and orderly after our month of chaos. We stayed in a heavenly suburban bungalow and I rested up. I was completely exhausted, and although not actually ill, could not have gone another mile on that bus. We had eaten hundreds of fried eggs on the journey as we had heard terrible stories of travellers dying of hepatitis, so didn't take any risks with food. We also could not literally afford to get sick as we had little money.

After a week's rest in Delhi I caught the train for Chennai, and for two days watched the sights of India pass by. I was alone now, and in a dreamy state of mind, happy just to sit there. From Chennai I got the bus down to Pondicherry, and as we came near the town I began to feel my breathing become strange and deep and an overwhelming energy pour into me. I saw a sign that said Jipmer and thought I must be there, but we went on a few more miles. At the bus terminus I stumbled out and got a rickshaw to the Ashram. It was Mother's darshan day and there were hundreds of people everywhere, but I pushed through to the front and immediately saw Shraddhavan standing there with Rod Hemsell and Big Jocelyn. A friend had given Shraddhavan a plane ticket and she had just arrived. I couldn't believe it. Mother came out onto the balcony and when I saw that tiny figure standing there I felt my old life had ended. The vibrations she gave out were beyond words. I felt taken care of from that very first minute.

After a few days I went to the Auroville office in Pondicherry and said, "I want to go to Auroville." They said OK, so I went and stayed with Shraddhavan in her hut. On my birthday I went to see Mother, waiting with hundreds of people holding flowers sitting on the stairs up to her room. We all shuffled slowly forward till we finally entered her room, and saw this tiny hunched figure in her nineties sitting on a chair. When it was my turn she looked right into my eyes, and time stopped and something cataclysmic happened inside me; I was never the same again. It was overwhelming and indescribable.

She got me, and I am still here, and there is no way I am ever leaving.

Talking to Judith after 36 years

I have had many incarnations here, and I am now starting a new one after being here for 36 years. I feel I need some time to think and just be after years of constant work. I feel this is very important for me right now. My house in Sri Ma down on the beach where I had lived for many years was smashed up by the tsumani three years ago, and now I live in a proper brick house in the security of Grace.

When I arrived here on August 15th, 1971, life was hugely primitive and deprived. We were surrounded by villages with absolutely no material prosperity, but I think at times they had more than we had. The heat never bothered me, and actually my girlhood dream came true when I became slim. I have always been a foodie, and so the deprivation did me good, though at the time I used to panic and think I was starving to death. Our breakfast was bran in hot water from the Ashram; lunch was red rice and ladies fingers, very heavy and tasteless; and in the evening we had Ashram bran and curd and jaggery. Many of us got boils, but in hippy folk lore it was just the toxins coming out. It was a hard time. Some people went home, but generally we were like a family of souls united by strong feelings of aspiration. We had no recourse to law in times of conflict and people just had to fight things out for themselves. (I personally never slashed anyone's tyres.) We used to call it "The Wild East" as it was so much like frontier times USA. Eventually the Indian government stepped in and told us we couldn't possibly have a Wild East here, as they expected something better from us, and they were supporting us in Mother's vision.

In 1984 my partner Gilles and I took our first holiday on a motor bike to the hills, and on my return Otto asked to talk to me and said, "Sit down. Ananda is quitting. We would like you to do the job at the Financial Service." Of course I agreed, and have been doing it ever since, until a few months ago. I enjoyed running the Auroville Fund, especially receiving the donations and feeling the generosity of so many well wishers all over the world. What could give more pleasure than receiving lots of money and being able to give it away and seeing Auroville grow with it?!

The situation has changed now, and I feel I don't have enough equanimity to work with the Financial Service any more. It is as if the whole world is drowning in bureaucracy and there is no way around it. The pressure from the Secretary and the Indian Government is getting more each year, and Mother has not given me the equanimity to cope with it, so I am leaving it for something else. Sometimes I feel it is Kali putting her big foot down.

I am absolutely sure that the Matrimandir is the heart of Auroville, as Mother said. We are still bickering about the details, but it totally doesn't matter, it is absolutely unimportant. Now the Matrimandir is finished and you can feel the completion, you can feel the power of all those years of work and inspiration. You can breathe it in. Life can get very difficult here when you feel up against everything. It is because you really care. The only thing I have learned over these 36 years is to understand that Mother is running things and she does it much better than you or I.

Judith

BHAGA ... WHO CAME FROM FRANCE IN 1972

In 1971 I was working as a teacher in France. We had a project with UNESCO to bring our students' attention to world hunger. They sent us big black and white posters that pictured starving people, and this had a powerful effect on me. (In my wildest dreams I wouldn't have believed that within one year I would be living amongst them!) We mounted a huge exhibition of these poor emaciated people interspersed with outrageous magazine pictures of greedy, over fed westerners. The shocking reality of our world made a great impression on everyone.

It hit something very deep within me, and I began to think about the awful world situation and what I could do about it. Although I had always felt that I was a mystical person since early childhood, I started to doubt the existence and the goodness of "God." I could see my future stretching comfortably and predictably in front of me; marriage, children, death. The programme did not appeal to me at all. I had no idea what to do with this life I had been given. I decided to make a pact with God, if he existed, and I gave him two years to fulfil it. I demanded that he show me why things are the way they are now, and in what way I could be involved in changing things for the better. Otherwise I could not see the point of being alive and would simply quit.

I had created a small group of students with enquiring minds to seek answers to such problems. We would look into various books and then report back to the group with anything we found helpful. Nothing much was ever revealed to us, and I could never find anything that would satisfactorily illuminate the reason for being alive.

Then one day a student knocked at my door excitedly clutching a big book called "The Life Divine" in French. The first twenty lines I read transformed my life. The first chapter seemed like an overture to a magnificent symphony, and I fell under its spell. The purpose of everything that existed was illuminated for me. All the pieces of the cosmic puzzle had come together. I said to God, "Thank you. I am definitely staying on now." Our little group rushed around and found a few other copies of Sri Aurobindo's books, and we began to practice the yoga of evolution to our best understanding. It seems very funny now looking back at that period. It was as if we were following a recipe book of how to do it, like a sort of spiritual gymnastics.

Three months later I invited a young Indian man who had grown up in the Ashram to show us some slides of somewhere called Auroville in South India. I was overwhelmed by it, and felt immediately that I had to go there. But I was very scared. I still remember one slide of Aspiration that horrified me. It showed scorched earth and a few huts and a terrible sun. It frightened me with its bleakness. I had never been remotely interested in India. I thought of it as a place where only the crazed hippies went. I thought to myself, "Why had Auroville been put in such a remote and wild place? Why hadn't it been put somewhere beautiful in Europe?"

When I told my parents of my plan to go there they were very afraid for me and appalled at my decision. My father had read something of Sri Aurobindo in his youth, but thought it was all about "concentrating on your navel and leaving the world behind." That is exactly the opposite of what Sri Aurobindo and the Mother's Integral Yoga is about!

For the first time in my life I was able to save some money, and within six months I joined four other friends on a chartered bus to Afghanistan. I would never have been able to go alone, I was too frightened, and I felt I was not capable of organizing the trip. Kabul was fascinating, as everything was totally new and fascinating to me, though I remember the heat was almost unbearable. I was very naive in 1972. The whole world of drugs was unknown to me; only the Divine Grace protected me from taking some, unaware of what it was that people were offering me everywhere. After a few months we got a third class sleeper train from Delhi to Madras, a rather uncomfortable but great few days.

I will never forget my first experience of Aspiration. I arrived at lunch time and was shown to the kitchen where people were eating. I could see at once that this was not a place of "peace and love." On the right side was a long high table where French and Italian people were talking and laughing loudly and eating very good French food. On the left were low tables where a few Germans were sitting in silence eating very simple vegetarian food. The two groups seemed to be looking at each other with self righteous contempt. I saw right away that even regarding food there were obviously two ways of doing things here; it would not be an easy ride! I almost ran away there and then, but knew I had to stay. I found a little room, but then fell sick with fever for a week and felt very confused and depressed.

At that time I had no idea of the lives of the Mother or Sri Aurobindo, but when Miriam (from the Boutique) asked me if I would like to go to Pondicherry on Mother's Darshan day on August 15th, I eagerly agreed. I remember seeing Mother as a tiny silhouette up on the balcony, as we were several streets away. It didn't make much of an impression on me at the time. I felt as if all my soul feelings were closed off and that my mind was made of iron. I thought it was ridiculous that all those flowers were given spiritual names, that westerners were worshipping this French woman ... everything seemed totally unacceptable to me.

The Grace of the Divine, however, soon managed to blow open my hard critical mind. I felt that my heart was opened wide again like it was in my childhood with my discovery of the Divine Mother.

I have hardly left Auroville in the last thirty years.

Talking to Bhaga after 37 years

I came to Auroville in 1972 and it was as if my whole inner motor became activated, with many tremendous inner experiences that the Divine Grace gave me. I experienced these profound truths without reading about them first. It was only afterwards that I read Sri Aurobindo and Mother's books and realized they were universal experiences. I worked in Matrimandir for a few years, and used to try and communicate with the public, who were very curious as to what the Matrimandir really was. The Indian people had never seen anything like this amazing building (then under construction) and automatically thought it was going to be a temple; the concept was completely new to them.

After a few years I used my teaching experience to try and organize some schooling for the children. It was very difficult at the time, but that was what I felt I really wanted to do. I wanted to communicate my experiences to others, especially to children who could not read about them.

This awareness was an unexpected development in my life, and my experiences at the cellular level showed me a new way of looking at the world. Because we received many books and periodicals from all over the world I began to realize that these experiences were becoming more and more common, they were not isolated any more, and because of this the planet's vibrations were changing. For quite a few years this topic was taboo in the Ashram, as it was thought that ordinary people could not experience these profound things, that only Mother could, but later they became more accepting.

This is what I came to Auroville for, not for the ecology or social experiment, but to be in the heart of a place where there was a collective dimension in this involvement. To Newcomers I would say the most important thing is to be willing to change and seek the unexpected in our personality. And to trust the Divine will do it for us; we only have to trust. All my activities and forms keep changing according to needs and finding a new way to function. In a practical way I try to manifest it by caring for the Repos community where I live and caring for the guests. This way of living takes a lot of patience and practice but it is a wonderful change. I know many people in Auroville live in the same way.

In 1985 it seemed very important that there should be a place where we could collect books that covered aspects of conscious evolution and scientific discoveries that were relevant. Aster gave us a little space in the Centre for Indian Studies and we set up a table with a few books. Later, we were given the

Bhaga

space that is now the Library of Evolution. It has become full to over flowing, and we need a larger space where we can hold activities.

I love to see the children growing up here – the first generation of "made in Auroville kids." I feel like an old aunty discreetly watching them grow up. They have a tremendous inner certitude and confidence. Although many of them do go through the usual intense teenage years, they emerge with an amazing self confidence. It is not like the kibbutz, where the kids leave, as the children here go abroad and return with skills they can offer to the community. They also do not have role models here. I think of all these different people here doing their own thing, all these different characters, so the children can choose their own influences,

For thirty years I had no family life to speak of as my family was in France. Then suddenly it changed, as I was asked to speak about my experiences in Europe. I got in contact with my French family and it was wonderful. I had to think carefully about how to explain my life to them, which was a good experience for me. I must have been successful, as my older sister actually came to live in Pondicherry for three years with her two children. So I had joyful invasions of my family on the week ends.

I continue to live my life in my house down by the ocean, doing the best I can, with the Divine's grace.

Bhaga passed away on 18th May 2022

B ... WHO CAME FROM USA IN 1974

A student in my class asked me about Sri Aurobindo. I said: "Sri who?" Later I checked with a friend at a nearby university. He said: "You shouldn't be teaching if you don't know Sri Aurobindo. He synthesized all yoga into an integral yoga, he was a founder of the freedom movement in India, he's a poet and mystic beyond what the world has ever seen. Educate yourself fast!"

I did. I could hardly believe the quality and truth of Sri Aurobindo's writings. In all my graduate studies, I had never come across such clarity, universality, and wisdom. His epic poem Savitri overwhelmed me. When I read an article announcing that a city was being built in India based on his thought --no question-- I had to be part of it. Immediately I began preparing and within a year I ended up in Auroville. I left everything including my girlfriends. I was returning to India, a country I had already visited two years before and dismissed as a hopeless mess that I thought would eventually self-destruct. Only later did I understand why the founder of Auroville affirmed: Auroville is in India because all the difficulties of the world are there but also all the solutions.

In 1958 when I enrolled in the University of San Francisco, I thought I knew practically everything. Very soon, I realized I was very wrong, but I didn't want the life I was supposedly being educated for. In 1959, a military history teacher tried boring me to death with his lecture. I was staring out the window to save myself, but he crept up behind me and screamed in my ear: "Wake up and piss boy, San Francisco is on fire!" Shocked and enlightened by that truth, I dropped out of the University. I hiked into the Trinity Alps Wilderness area of California. Alone, I climbed a high mountain and sat on a rock to talk to God. There had to be a way to save myself and the world.

The Peace Corps hadn't been invented yet. There was no flower power or hippies yet. With my Catholic background, the best thing I could come up with was to become a Jesuit priest. The education was intense but soul-satisfying until the hypocrisy of the institution became too obvious. Then I had to speak up ("you are a heretic") and be dismissed, but the experience educated me for Auroville in ways I never expected. The theology and philosophy opened me for Sri Aurobindo. Living in a global monastic community prepared me for the multi-cultural collective of Auroville.

When I arrived in Auroville in 1974, it didn't match my expectations at all. The articles I had read and people I talked with had given me a different impression. The harsh living conditions, the climate, the poverty of the environment, the lack of electricity and

(B) Bill, Francis, Robi

water, the abundance of mosquitoes and flies and all the rest seemed to much to take. I quickly realized that only a spiritual sense of the vision and Dream proposed by the Mother who founded Auroville could make it possible to live here. When I arrived she had just passed away. Her passing unleashed the forces she had previously controlled. A battle ensued between the residents and those who tried to impose another vision on Auroville rather than the human unity we had come for. It was a traumatic time for Auroville but I survived because Marcia from Brazil loved me. I also changed myself from being Bill into B. Just the name change of symbolically getting the "ill" out of my name helped. In 1980 the Parliament of India passed the Auroville Emergency Provisions Act that saved the situation by making Auroville legally belong to Humanity and managed by the residents.

Talking with B after 49 years

The best decision I ever made was to join Auroville but did I really make such a decision? I feel my soul knew its destiny and grace arranged the circumstances to make it happen. I am ever grateful that my life in Auroville has also been centered around Matrimandir, the soul of the City. This concrete aspiration of humanity for the Divine and the Divine's response is a mystery of love. This is the energy of the Mother, Mother Earth, Mother Nature, Mother India. This love creates and sustains us, the Cosmos, and what more could be said?

FRANZ ... WHO CAME FROM GERMANY IN 1974

I was born in a small town in Germany just after the war. Half the population were Catholics and the other half Protestant and everyone went to church on Sunday. This world was divided in two, but I never saw any contradiction between these two aspects of Christianity; I just took it for granted, as children do. I was later sent to a very traditional Benedictine monastery boarding school, but I remember always feeling a strong pull to Eastern religions. I don't know where this attraction came from. At that time there were few books and little information about these sort of things available. But I always had this fascination for China and Japan and the Far East.

I went to art school in my teens, and had a wonderful time exploring different cultures. Life was very different forty years ago. It was easy to cross borders, as there were no guns or terrorists then. I travelled around Algeria and Morocco, and later by bus through Iran and Pakistan. I was amazed by the traditional life of these countries; how the women were always out of sight, how hospitable the people were to a complete stranger. I went up to Bangladesh and Nepal and travelled around by train, bus and plane; there were no Lonely Planet guide books in those days. I even went to Somalia and Mogadishu, places that are only known nowadays for their lawlessness and war. We travelled then by way of a Messageries Maritimes ship travelling from Yokohama in Japan to Marseille in France.

I returned to Germany and got a good job and a beautiful apartment, but I couldn't settle down to the materialistic way of life anymore. It was then the sixties, and everyone was experimenting with drugs and meditation. A Japanese Roshi called Nagaya came to Germany to give classes in Zen, and I was fascinated by him. My first experience of meditation opened up a completely new world to me. (I was later surprised to find out how many people in Auroville had been influenced by him.)

After three years of working as a graphic designer I wanted to explore the world again, but I had no clear idea of where to go. War was still raging with East Pakistan and there were no flights available to India, so I decided to go to Mexico and began to learn Spanish. Just as I was packing for this trip the travel agent rang me and said flights had just re-opened for India, and did I still want to go? I was very excited by this news and booked to Rishikesh, where I saw Guru Maharaji of Divine Light and other celebrated teachers. Rishikesh at that time was full of gurus and rishis, and it seemed to me like a spiritual super market, though I felt no particular attraction to any of them.

On the plane from Frankfurt to Cairo I had been talking to a German fellow passenger who was on his way to Pondicherry. He told me what a great lady the Mother was, and that one could go and actually stay in the Ashram where she lived and have an interview with her. He explained that I could write to the Mother and enclose a photograph of myself. (In those days Mother chose you by deeply looking at your eyes in the photo.) I did this immediately, and was at first very disappointed when I didn't get a reply from her personally. Instead, her secretary – it was then her son André – suggested that I talk to people in Germany first and read the recommended books that would be an entry into the yoga.

I was introduced to Eckhard, one of the first Germans to come and visit the Ashram, and he had a great influence on me. Another was Heinz Kappes, who was a Protestant priest who had to leave Germany during the war and went to live in Jerusalem. He had started there reading and translating "Life Divine" and other books from Sri Aurobindo and the Mother, and he started later, very carefully, introducing Sri Aurobindo's ideas into his church sermons. I found this fascinating.

Eventually I was able to take one year's leave from my job, and came to Pondicherry. It was the most spectacular year of my life. Medhananda was the German director of the Ashram library, and every afternoon at 4 p.m. he would meet visitors. This was a very beautiful and gentle way of introducing Ashram life, and I was enormously impressed with his intellect and understanding. He had been a lawyer in Germany, then fled the Nazis and lived for years on a coffee and vanilla plantation on Morea - Tahiti.

In those days Ashram life was very simple and beautiful as there were no distractions; there was absolutely nowhere else to go, not that I wanted to. I was blissfully happy to eat in the Ashram dining room and follow the daily routine and be surrounded by these remarkable people. Mother was in the last year of her life at that time, and I had one meeting with her. I did two books of drawings of her and Sri Aurobindo and presented them to her. She looked carefully through the books and gave me a beautiful smile. Darshan days were eagerly awaited and they felt like a child's Christmas Day with Mother's appearance on the balcony. I had the greatest good fortune to attend four of these darshans and experience her concentration of amazing energy. I felt as if I was in the middle of the universe and the energy was spreading out all over the world.

But all too quickly my year-long leave came to an end. I had to return to Germany. On the very night I was flying from Bombay to Cairo Mother left her body. I was sitting on the plane, and someone gave me an English newspaper and I read about it. I was terribly shocked. Many of the Ashramites had somehow expected her not to leave her body, and hoped for some sort of miracle. Some people wondered if the Ashram would be able to continue without her presence and guiding light, or would disintegrate. I personally found the level of energy there so high with the living Mother there, that I couldn't imagine it being the same – which of course it wasn't. The sheer scale and concentration of power during Mother's presence could be very much felt, and blockages and resistances in us used to cause headaches and the like. Although I was very happy there, I couldn't imagine spending the rest of my life working in the Ashram Dining Hall. I was looking for something else.

One day I had gone to visit Auroville, and was amazed at that big hole of the future Matrimandir. I knew that one day there would be a city here and I definitely wanted to be part of it. I went to Auroville Press and volunteered my graphic skills, then went and found a house in the next community, Fraternity, where I have been ever since. I felt as if I had absolutely fallen on my feet.

Mother had given me an invitation to come to Auroville, and she formulated it so strongly no one could ever refuse it. "Will you participate?" she had asked me. "A new world is coming; are you ready?"

I was indeed ready.

Talking to Franz after 34 years

I was very moved by something a visitor recently said to me. She told me how envious she was of our way of life here in Auroville, as we have a vision to live by – "as if you are following a star." I realized how true that was, and without that star my life would be very lacking in direction. Being aware of the star gives me a certain contentment, and I can face my day to day problems with a sense of purpose and steadiness. I need to be constantly reminded of this direction, and the Savitri Study Group I go to on Sunday mornings always puts me back in the spirit of the great vision of Sri Aurobindo and the Mother. It is always a joy to read and meditate upon Savitri in our small intimate group.

I have been here since 1974. In Germany I trained as a graphic artist, and I try to use these skills in my work and bring beauty to exhibitions, presentations, or just providing lunch at Aurelec for the staff and guests. Aurelec was one of the first units in the beginning of the 1980s, and I joined it at the beginning and have been there ever since. I have also lived in nearby Fraternity all that time. I built a little house there and that has been my life. The units in Fraternty were flourishing with about 200 people working there doing weaving and making lampshades for Oxfam; it was an exciting time.

This summer I went to Germany for a couple of months, and on my return I very clearly realized that even the very small contribution to the whole that I have made here is very worth while. The world seems to be moving towards more and more conflicts and wars and devastation, and I think it will get much worse in the future. Here in Auroville we feel we are contributing something very valuable. I feel that Mother has set us a sort of computer programme that if you try to follow it can never disappoint. But we have to remember it. She used to send Auroville big cards in envelopes with beautiful words of encouragement handwritten on them. They are still valid for us. One day I would like to do an exhibition of them and put them in a book.

One thing does disturb me, however. I spent some time in hospital in Germany and had lots of time to think about what we usually block out – the fact that we are all getting older, and what is death, and how are we going to face it, or how are we preparing ourselves for it? This is also here still a topic that not many want to face or talk about. In the next 10 years there will be quite a lot of the old-timers here who will be in their seventies and eighties. It will be a big challenge

Franz

for the community. Many of us live alone and have no supportive family. We need to make many more arrangements now for the aging population who have given so much to Auroville, and not wait until it is a matter of urgency. It needs to be given priority, and not get tucked away in the hope that aging will never happen.

When I first came to Auroville and saw the big hole for Matrimandir I was amazed by the idea that here in a kind of desert would one day stand a marvellous 'globe'. What a struggle it has been! It is a miracle! We had nothing at that time, no money and few skills. Nothing but a dedicated belief, but everything came together like in a puzzle.

I feel Auroville, and especially the Matrimandir, is a very positive contribution we have already made for India and the world.

GILLIAN ... WHO CAME FROM AUSTRALIA IN 1977

I grew up in a normal suburban family, and nothing much happened until I was sixteen, when I met my first "real" person. It was 1968, the time of the counter culture, and I met this man who to me seemed like the only complex, searching person I had ever met. One evening he took me to dinner in a beautiful artist's house, and during the meal a goat, or a sheep, I can't remember which, walked in and wandered about then made a mess on the floor, and nobody turned a hair. I was very impressed by this, quite blown over in fact, as it was utterly unthinkable in my family house. I later told my mother about it, and she rather sarcastically said: "Well, now you know how the other half lives." My immediate response was, " But I am the other half!"

This man knew about Auroville, and told me of an old French lady who lived in an Ashram. In 1974 I travelled to South East Asia, but didn't really enjoy being there as in those days foreigners were not common and I was always stared at and hassled. For some reason the culture did not really interest me. I remember going to a Sikh temple on Guru Nanek's birthday in Singapore, and being fascinated by the Indian clothes, the huge cauldrons full of dhal, the buckets of food served on banana leaves, and something there spoke to me. I felt a fascination, an enchantment with India. I loved the soft Indian cotton scarves that everyone was wearing, the subtle feel and smell of their material, and I wanted to go there.

For the first few days in Calcutta I was terrified to go out of the hotel and stayed in my room, but one morning I went out very early before the crowds were on the streets and something very strange happened to me. I felt as if the sights and sounds of India were touching and opening my heart, as if my soul was awakening to India. Something in me relaxed, and the tension I felt I had always been carrying just melted away. Until then I could never see the point of being alive; there seemed to be no reason for it.

I then went to see a guru in North India, but I got tired of being cold, remembered my friend who lived in Auroville, and decided to come south to get warm and take a look at Auroville. I lived in Pondicherry for a year and had some deep experiences, read Savitri and wrote poetry, and came to visit Auroville occasionally. I felt very drawn to it, and remember thinking: "Thank God someone thought of this place."

I felt as if I had discovered why I had been born. All the questions I had ever asked, and even the ones I hadn't thought of, were answered here, and in 1977 I came to live here.

Gillian

Talking to Gillian after 30 years

When I first came, 30 years ago, I lived down on Far Beach, now called Sri Ma, but I felt very isolated and so soon moved up to Sincerity. I met Lila, who was a weaver, and I remember I was wearing a pair of crocheted shoes and she showed me how to make them. That was the beginning of our partnership, with a production workshop making crochet and beaded items like bags, wallets and wall hangings. After a while Lila moved back to the USA, and I continued the unit and sold the products in the Pondicherry Auroville Boutique, which I have been doing ever since for the last 30 years. That has been my anchor in Auroville.

I have always been involved with making cycle paths as I love to cycle, and even years ago the traffic was building up and I thought we must make some alternatives. People have helped over the years, but now it is mainly Alok and I who keep on with it. The cycle paths are so important, and more and more so each year.

My involvement with the village of Kuilapalayam down at the other end of Auroville has been an ongoing affair. For my first few years here I never went there, just sped through it occasionaly on my bike as fast as possible. It was only when the Health Centre asked me to landscape their grounds that I noticed what a terrible mess the village was in; there was garbage everywhere and the drains were overflowing and there were no toilets. I really felt I wanted to get involved, and got two toilets built, and to this day I am still involved with trying to keep them clean. It felt good to be involved and to be of use, and I had a good relationship with the leaders, and the villagers were very appreciative. Nowadays the village has changed enormously; it has become almost urban and affluent and it is impossible to make an impact in the same way.

Kuilapalayam has quite a lot of Auroville land, and I have always felt that a development on this land could be a marvellous connection between the two. As it is now, there is little connection except between individuals. It would be a marvellous opportunity for the tamarind grove near the Bakery to be used as a public market place with shops and a plaza and a volleyball court for the boys – so much potential – but the project was blocked by the Land people and it will eventually be sold for house plots. Its lack of vision is stunning. Auroville by its prosperity has created the gangs, the "goondas" of the village, that cause regular murders, and it must take steps to rectify the situation for these young and frustrated village men. What will help to change the situation there? Surely not another five Kashmiri shops!

My experience of the Tamil people is of a very tolerant and non-judgemental people. They always gave me a lot of freedom to make a big mess, and never held it against me. Most Aurovilians are insulated from them, and this creates an impression of "breakdown" and lack of communication. I have always had a living relationship with them, as I have always worked with them and hugely enjoyed it. For example, many Tamils are working at the new Pour Tous, and as everyone has the same goals it all works well together. I still only speak "baby Tamil" but when the new Language Lab. opens at this end I am definitely going to finally master it. Language is such a divide here; nearly all my friends are German, and when they socialize I am not included, as they like to speak German, a behaviour pattern which I can understand.

About my future? I am an astrologer, but I never think about it. One thing I do know however is that soon Pluto is moving into Capricorn, and a big change with a lot of oppression is due, and this concerns me.

JOY ... WHO CAME FROM PONDICHERRY ASHRAM IN 1977.

I had the unbelievable grace to live in the Pondicherry Ashram from the age of six to twenty three. My grandmother admired Sri Aurobindo, and when I was six years of age she insisted that my father and his brother send their oldest children to be educated in the Ashram school.
I think my poor mother was upset, but in those days the authority of the husband's mother was undisputed. It was decided that we would stay with our grandmother, who would care for us. I still remember the long train journey down to Pondicherry, feeling very excited if somewhat apprehensive.
As soon as we got there we were taken to the beach. I had never seen the sea before, and I can still remember the feeling of that vast expanse of space and water; it made a great impression on me. I lived in a little room with my grandmother and began my life of routine and order. I used to see Mother often, either at the balcony darshans, or more often in the school, which she would often visit. Mother loved children, and we were always getting dressed up for her and making paper hats, and she encouraged and applauded us. I remember on my seventh birthday going up to her to receive my little bag of seven sweets which she playfully dangled in front of me. She had an air of quiet intensity and purpose, as if she was utterly concentrating on who was in front of her. Everyone loved her.
After a year I became ill; I think I had been too young to leave home and my grandmother was too busy with the Ashram life to give me enough care, so my father came and took me back home to Kolkatta. I stayed there for a year but wanted to come back, and when a teacher, Animi, who was Nolini's secretary, offered to look after me my father brought me down on the train again. I lived happily with her for two years, then was offered a place in the Ashram boarding school. These were the best years of my life.

I always felt very supported and cared for by everyone, as if I was part of a very big family. Mother believed in order and regularity and oversaw every aspect of our daily lives, and our days were full, creative and joyful. Our classes ran from 7.45 a.m. to 11.30 a.m., and then we had lunch and went home to rest until 2.30. In the afternoon we had classes in our mother tongues, then at 4 p.m. a snack before sports. Mother always gave great importance to sports. She believed they should be given as much emphasis as lessons, as in integral education the body, mind and spirit were of equal importance and should be well balanced. Although we had competitions they were not held in a competitive way, but in a manner to develop our spirit of aiming at perfection, to struggle to go beyond our limits.

Mother emphasized that there was no difference between girls and boys, and we should not think in those terms until we were 16. We used to wear shorts, which for the locals was a great novelty, if not a scandal. Our parents had complete faith and trust in Mother and never interfered, and so let her permit us to ride around on our bicycles in shorts. As a teenager I remember a feeling of laziness, or maybe it was just tamas, as we were growing so quickly. Mother completely ignored this, no indulgence at all, and we had to run and jump as before.

We had freedom as teenagers to be seen with boy friends, which was very rare in India in those days. The atmosphere in the

Joy

Ashram was so sustaining that sexuality was never such a big problem as it was in the outside world. And the Mother's strong presence was always there with us.

I remember falling in love at 14. The emotions were so overwhelming and unfamiliar I did not know what was happening to me. Mother always invited us to write to her if we had any problems, and so in desperation I did write and she replied: "At this point the best thing to do is concentrate on your development." I foolishly didn't follow her advice, and had three years of emotional turmoil.

We had ample opportunities to follow our natural tendencies and gifts, as our teachers were people who were passionate about their subjects. We sometimes had foreigners who were well qualified in the arts or a language, and Mother put them in places where they could serve us best. Everyone studied everything till the age of 15, so all our basic needs were covered, and our parents financially contributed whatever they could. I became passionate about singing and dancing and had an excellent training, which is the background of my work today, twenty five years later .

I finished the Ashram school at the age of 21 with the equivalent of a B.A. but stayed on for another two years and worked in different departments. Mother believed it was good for people involved in the arts to do something practical, "to get your nose in matter," and so I was put, to my initial horror, in house maintenance. My work was to update the inventories of the "godowns", the huge storage rooms, which had probably never been done before. Actually it proved very good for me, as I learned to work with people and develop the practical side of my nature.

In 1977 I met Jean, who helped with the Ashram theatre and lived in Aspiration in Auroville, and I used to go there and visit him. Auroville at that time seemed to me like theatre in real life, full of fire and wild spirit and humour. A group of us from the Ashram used to come out on a bus after sports and help with the concreting at Matrimandir . I thought it was all very inspiring, if a little crazy.

One day I had this very strange feeling, more a direct awareness. I suddenly felt "This is my place". It was as if a page had been turned. I didn't know if it was a good or a bad thing, I was just very surprised.

Every so often I ask myself, "Is this still my place?" And the answer is still "Yes."

TIM ... WHO CAME FROM LONDON IN 1977

I first came to Auroville 'Out of Africa' — to use Isak Dinesen's book title

My wife and I had decided to take a year's sabbatical with our two children, then aged 6 and 3½, and travel down through Africa to Capetown; ship across the Indian Ocean to Bombay; and see parts of India and Nepal before returning overland again to London. For this we bought a new Land-Rover, and converted it to sleep all four of us inside. It became, for us, literally a home on wheels.

Before we left London an Italian friend of ours told us to visit Auroville in India, which he described as a place where people from many nations were working together in peace and harmony. Something about his words inspired us, and so we put it on our itinerary.

He was Mother's first "messenger".

On leaving Bombay we headed south to first visit a Canadian woman living in a Tibetan refugee settlement near Goa. However, the road south was terrible. For hundreds of kilometres every bridge was down for a massive road widening scheme, and we had to drive through rocky, dusty riverbeds each time. We felt like turning back north, but decided to first ask the Canadian woman for advice. She was amazing; she had never seen Auroville, but she encouraged us to go on and visit the place.

She was Mother's second "messenger".

On arrival in Pondy we were directed out past JIPMER to an unsigned turn-off into the countryside. We then drove for kilometre after kilometre on dusty tracks – through a village (Edayanchavady) and past a nice looking house (Auroson's Home) – but nowhere could we see any sign of a township; just a couple of unimpressive buildings in the distance near a large tree. We decided to ask there for directions, but just short of the tree the engine began making a terrible screeching noise, and we had to come to a halt in the mid-day sun.

I couldn't imagine a worse situation in which to break down, but what happened next was extraordinary. When I went over to the nearby buildings, literally the first man I spoke to was a mechanic. It seemed miraculous, so I explained that we were broken down near the tree, which we now saw was a banyan.

"We're looking for Auroville," I said.

"This is Auroville," he replied.

"No," I went on, "I mean the city of Auroville."

"You're in the city," he said. "Although it's not yet built, you're at the very heart of the city area at a place called the Matrimandir."

25,000 kilometres of travel, and we had broken down for the first and only time just 50 metres from the absolute centre of Auroville! Not only had we broken down, but I next saw that we also had a bad leak from the petrol tank, and then our daughter said she was feeling sick! We had been well and truly brought to a complete halt by circumstances beyond our control and comprehension.

That was 15th March 1973. Ten days later we kneeled before The Mother in her room for her blessings. It proved to be an incredible grace, because a week later she stopped seeing any new people.

We stayed for 7 weeks, working most of the time in the horticultural nursery, but also to experience Mother's April Darshan. Then, after visiting Nepal, we returned overland to Europe via Pakistan, Afghanistan, Iran and Turkey to complete a year of travel.

We had done over 40,000 kms and had our passports stamped by 25 countries, but more important was the stamp on our hearts and psyche made by The Mother and Auroville.

When we left Auroville to begin our long journey back to the UK, I had felt that we were actually leaving 'home'; a home to which I wanted to return.

With Mother's help I finally did in 1977, this time " Out of England".

GEORGES ... WHO CAME FROM BELGIUM IN 1979

I was brought up as a Catholic, like everybody else at the place I come from, my "native place". I enjoyed enormously being a choir boy, except for having to get up so early. Later I studied at an institute run by priests. There I learned to play the piano and especially the organ. I would play the organ for hours, all alone high in the big space of an often dark church. If I remember correctly, I must have played the organs of seventeen different churches.

My future brother-in-law was the direct cause of my losing my faith. He was a militant liberal, and for the first time I heard via him something different from the teachings of the priests. I was also very much interested in occultism, and when this leaked out the priests regarded me with suspicion. Eventually, after seven years of studying with them, I was given the choice: leave or be thrown out. They never showed any degree of concern for me. I am still somewhat bitter about that. On the other hand, their institution was the best I could have been in, for there was music, theatre practice, artistic shows, (censured) films and sports.

I had to earn a living, and my liberal brother-in-law found me a job at the Magistrate Court in Ghent. To live in a big town was at first a disorienting experience. But Ghent is a very beautiful town which has kept its medieval centre intact, and it would become the city of my heart. I had to join the army for obligatory military service, and became a second-lieutenant in the infantry, commanding a platoon of heavy mortars. The army was a dreary affair, but it gave me a thorough physical training and experience in much that, many years later, would be useful for writing "Hitler and His God".

After my military service I returned to Ghent and my job as a clerk of the court. I thought I would go mad with boredom among the stacks of files and the cultural empty-headedness. I became known as a poet at that time, and through a concatenation of coincidences got involved in the local theatre life. At that time there appeared out of nowhere very small semi-professional theatres in many Flemish towns. The theatre, like the circus, always had a strange attraction for me – it may have something to do with its particular scent of make-up, old clothes and cavernous dark spaces behind the scenery, and with the presence of women in circumstances different from everyday life. My first play was performed, successfully, when I was twenty-four.

When, again through my liberal brother-in-law, I got a job as a supervisor in a school for teachers, I was saved from becoming mad as a court clerk. The job provided me with much free time, and even on the job I had plenty of time to read. Together with my activities as a poet and a playwright, I practically every day went on some assignment as a local journalist for the press, and I had a weekly programme on the radio.

One day, a professional theatre company was founded to play the big theatre between the belfry and the cathedral in Ghent. Strange to say, on one of my visits there, years before, I had had an almost painfully strong feeling that some time in the future my destiny would lie in that theatre. And indeed, I became the dramaturg of the new company and would end up as the artistic manager. (A "dramaturg" is the man in charge of the literary aspect of a repertory company.) I saw some two hundred performances per year, in our own theatre and elsewhere, and on one occasion counted the talks I had given in the past season: seventy-five. But having to distribute the parts, and by so doing intervening in the careers of twenty-three king-size egos, is no sinecure. And as a manager you never enter your theatre without at least one serious problem awaiting you.

Somewhere in the autumn of 1964, after having been at the late show of a cinema, I stopped, as was my habit, in front of the window of a bookshop. There I saw a newly published book, "Sri Aurobindo, ou l'aventure de la conscience". Although religion, and certainly India, did not belong within my horizon, "something" told me to buy that book. The next morning it was the first thing I did. French books at the time were still bound in a way that you had to cut them open. After cutting the first pages, I read a quotation from Sri Aurobindo saying that a person could become anything he felt like, for God was in him. Something indescribable happened at the top of my head, and that is why I am here.

I started reading anything I could find in connection with Indian and Eastern spirituality, quite chaotically. And I started meditating and practising some hatha-yoga postures, usually after midnight, when I came home after my rather worldly occupations. I was given the necessary experiences which supported me in my lonely search. For more than five years I lived in that way. Two times I tried to talk about what really occupied my mind, once with a director and once with a set designer, who I thought were my friends. In both cases the reaction was uproarious laughter.

I felt less and less at home in the theatre where I was working. I had long ago discovered that behind all their airs the actors were very petty bourgeois, and so also were my colleagues in management. The call to go to India became ever stronger. At long last I quit my enviable position, played the guide on touring buses through Western Europe during one season, and when I had been swung around sufficiently in that way, bought a plane ticket to India. I didn't know whether the Mother was still alive, and imagined the Ashram as a white building under a blue sky, with a tall palm tree next to it.

My nearest relatives didn't realise what a step this was for me. For many months I had been travelling all the time, so they thought that this was another one of my trips. But I felt in my heart that, although I told myself that this was only a visit, I was leaving them for good. And to their amazement I burst out crying above my fried eggs on the eve of my departure.

Having arrived in Pondicherry after a rather traumatic journey – India thirty-seven years ago was not how it is today – and having deposited my luggage in a hotel at the sea-side, my first steps were directed towards that Ashram, with my jacket slung over my shoulder. I expected a building with a big gate, and having seen a picture of the Samadhi, I expected to see the small tiled roof behind it. But as at first I had not been brought farther than the entrance, I kept walking around the Ashram for three days (not continuously!), asking everybody I met where it was and not believing them. At long last someone accompanied me around the corner of the reading room, and there I saw the Samadhi and the tiled roof behind it. I had finally arrived.

I have described my first visit to the Mother and the power of her public darshans elsewhere. I had the privilege of meeting her personally several times. I stayed in the Ashram for eight years. In the meantime I became acquainted with most of the first Aurovilians, some of whom came to consult me about their horoscope. And it was while calculating a horoscope that an inner voice told me to move to Auroville. As this was at the time of the "events", it was not easy to acquiesce. By that time, however, I had read more of Sri Aurobindo and the Mother's writings, and I knew that one cannot disobey an 'adesh' except at one's peril. And see, I am still here.

Talking to Georges after 30 years

What had brought me to India were the ideals of Auroville, yet I stayed eight years in the Ashram. The reason was quite simply that I would not have been able to live in Auroville in that early stage of its existence, for the circumstances were really primitive, and one can only have the greatest admiration for the first courageous people who chose to settle in the City of the Future. Except for the urn and the amphitheatre there was nothing but a couple of sheds in the Centre. Then were was Forecomers with Bob and Deborah, Utility with Mali, Certitude with Frederick and Shyama, one or two huts in the Green Belt, and the first huts in Aspiration, in what was still open goat country. In the beginning of 1970 it was possible to lose one's way when going down from Aspiration, through the fields, to Chinnamudaliarchavady on what is now the East Coast Road. It may now sound hardly believable, but at that time the centre of the activities in connection with Auroville was Promesse in Morattandi, on the Tindivanam road.

When I wrote to the Mother for an occupation, she made me a physical education coach with the New Groups. These were the newly arrived children and the special cases, some of them thrown out of the regular groups. They were all ages, from six to twenty-two. I still see myself walking the very first time in the Nandanam garden holding on each side the hand of a tiny tot and feeling foolish. But the Mother knew what was good for me, of course, and gradually I learned to understand the reason behind it all. I continued being a sports coach for four years, after which I began to translate the first of the twelve or thirteen books I have translated into Dutch.

In the meantime I studied astrology, and several other divinatory arts, very seriously. Before long I was consulted not only by Ashramites but also by outsiders. If I had wanted I could have become a rich man by asking the fees most would pay willingly. By this time the Auroville population had increased and my renown as an astrologer spread there too. And this is how I met many future fellow Aurovilans, especially from the French speaking population. I also met many of them when taking visitors to Auroville.

Then came the moment that, while calculating a horoscope, an inner voice told me to go and live in Auroville. This was a tough decision to make, for the girl who is still my partner wanted to stay in the Ashram. But when you receive the command, there is no gainsaying. And so, behind the bullock cart which carried my scarce furniture and my books, I cycled to Auroville through a Pondicherry in full festive mood, for it was the eve of the Mother's centenary.

Many of my acquaintances in the Ashram did not forgive my move; some of them talked to me again only after twenty-five years, others never have. What made the decision still tougher was the fact that it happened in full "events", the painful separation of Auroville from the Sri Aurobindo Society, and that much of this happened in a rather fanatic atmosphere.

Friends had seen to it that a hut was built in Aspiration, a hexagonal one-brick wall and a keet roof. There I lived for twelve years. I soon became involved in the revived Last School, where I had some excellent years teaching children who are now having their own children. In the meantime I continued translating and sometimes functioning as the football referee of rather recalcitrant sportsmen. On the very day I wanted to start the preparatory work for my own first book, I had a severe heart attack. Having survived the attack, I taught for about three years young village children in New Creation, which was an endearing experience. And when that was no longer possible for health reasons, I became a full-time student and writer – which I am to this day .

Georges

George van Vrekhem passed away on 31st August 2012.

AURALEE... WHO CAME FROM CANADA IN 1981.

I grew up in Vancouver, Canada. My mother had always been interested in India; I don't know why, perhaps it was because she read a lot and somehow it had caught her imagination.

When I was 14 I used to enjoy going to the local Anglican church, because I loved the stained glass windows and the beautiful voice of the minister. One day I rashly asked the minister, "Do you believe in God?" "No," he answered me, and I was devastated. How could he be there, conducting services every evening, if he didn't believe in God? I ran to my mother, crying, feeling disillusioned, and stayed away from churches for almost twenty years.

As an adult, my sister was searching for something else, always reading and searching for meaning. One day she showed me Sri Aurobindo's "The Life Divine"; it had made a great impression on her, so I immediately started to read it. My reaction to page one was, "Oh my God!" I had just completed a master's degree at McGill University in "The Teaching of Reading", and just one attempt at the first twenty-line sentence daunted me. I closed the book, not to open it again for two years!

My sister had heard that Sri Chinmoy was going to speak in New York, so we drove down to see him. She had discovered Sri Aurobindo's Centenary Edition in the McGill University library, and we read "Savitri" aloud during the eight hour drive; it was wonderful!

Sri Chinmoy was magnificent in his turquoise silk dhoti, my favourite colour, and I was absolutely spellbound by the simplicity of this cross-legged seated figure. I had never seen anyone like him before.

In December 1981, my sister decided to go to India to see where Sri Aurobindo and the Mother had lived. Three months later, I went to the Montreal airport to meet her flight home. I took one look at her, and saw a peace and silence which

I'd never seen before in her eyes. I thought, "If you can change so much in three months, I'm going there!"

My marriage had ended a year before, and so I was free to embark on a new experience with my three young children. I made a sort of contract with God: 'If You want me to go, have one of my children accepted by the Ashram school.' The chances seemed very slim, but miraculously my 3 year-old was accepted into the Ashram kindergarten, and so I started to make my preparations.

My apartment lease was coming up for renewal, so I decided not to renew it and to sell all my possessions. My cousins bought some of my nicest furniture and then I put an advert in the paper to sell the rest. I didn't get a single answer for days, and I was beginning to despair, when a man who had just returned from Mexico with a large family came and bought every single thing, all the bits and pieces of family life.

I bought a return one-year ticket on the very first Air India flight from Montreal to Delhi. It was Gandhiji's birthday, and there were a lot of VIPs celebrating the inaugural flight with champagne. I was finally off!

My first Indian shock was when the man at the Customs told me I would have to pay quite a lot of money on my stereo system, as it was new. I looked shocked, so he very kindly suggested I say it was 5 years old. I agreed to do so, but when the Customs officer came back, I thought, 'How can I start a new life at the Ashram with a lie? What sort of people were these?'

I was overwhelmed by the sights and smells of India, and looking back I see some of my preconceptions were very naïve. The first half dozen Ashramites I met spoke Gujarati, so I studied it for three hours every day, not realizing that a completely different language, Tamil, was spoken in Pondicherry. The local people had great difficulty in understanding my North American English. And I remember going to the bicycle shop to get cycles for my kids, and when the man was talking to me and I didn't recognize it as English, I thought it was some sort of Indian dialect. There was no TV, no English radio in those days, and the local people had had very little exposure to English.

The practical difficulties of organizing three children to fit in with Ashram life was pretty demanding. Keeping them immaculate like the Indian children at the Ashram school, trying to get them to eat Ashram food with its repetitious meals... the list sometimes felt endless. I was advised to give them eggs and protein foods as the little boy got bad heat rash and we all began to lose weight. The worst for me to deal with were the ants and cockroaches. The ants would constantly march up the wall, and the nights were spent in dread of giant, unkillable cockroaches.

The family eventually settled down and the children loved being here.

I remember the feeling I'd had back in Canada that I couldn't talk about God to anyone. I couldn't talk to anyone about anything that really mattered to me. I'd felt I was leading a double life, and now I could be myself.

When I was in Pondicherry I remember seeing women on big dusty motorbikes from Auroville. I thought how tough life must be for them, and how I could never live like that. I went to visit Auroville, and was surprised by the Aurovilians' hostility to me. I asked if I could eat at the Centre kitchen and was told "No."

I asked where I could buy a loaf of bread, and nobody would tell me where the bakery was. This was the time of "the troubles," and they saw me as an Ashramite.

AuroCulture kept asking me to visit her 'school', but I never felt very enthusiastic, and it took me one and a half years to finally get there. I took the bus to Udavi School and walked into the school and looked at the Tamil children there sitting on the ground. I felt blown away by the consciousness in their eyes. I immediately said I would volunteer to help out the teachers there. I started off

Auralee

doing one day a week, then soon did five days, and my two children who were still waiting for a place in the Ashram school accompanied me and were very happy there.

Maggie eventually asked me if I would take over the school, and that is how we came to live in Auroville. I used to come to Matrimandir every night and just sit there under the stars and gaze at the huge construction. I could feel the power of it, as if it was calling me for the rest of my life.

At first I was a little taken aback by the wild Aurovilian children and wondered how my kids would be able to cope with them and integrate into Auroville life.

In 1985 Auroville held an International Year of the Child conference, and Auroville children were speaking. Someone asked a girl of about 14 what she thought the purpose of Auroville was, and she answered: "Transformation." Somehow this child's answer went right to my heart, and I knew we were in the right place.

Talking to Auralee after 12 years

In my 12 years here since my arrival on Mother's birthday in 1996 many changes have happened in me. It has been a kind of mixed thing, but I guess the most difficulties have always been with myself ... how to change, how to let go, how to surrender more. Basically, I have been happy in Auroville, and sometimes very happy. Now and then I see signs of progress in myself, and that is always reassuring. This year some disturbing things happened, and I realised that just a few years ago I would have been very shaken, but this time around I felt some equanimity, almost like a still lake ... nothing moved in me. One day I remember just sitting looking out of my window at the beautiful trees, and had an overwhelming sense of gratitude. For about six months I felt a sort of bliss, day after day.

It has been a daily challenge to drop the old stuff, the feeling that you "know something." I now realise there are as many truths as there are people and each one is doing the best he can. A lot of people are doing beautiful things in Auroville. Over the years I can see the change in them; it reflects in their faces. I am so glad Matrimandir is finished, I can see all the work and care and love that has gone into its making. Its beauty is extraordinary. And it is there for every one of us. When I go "out of station" I get itchy for "that look in the eyes". Here we have something, an authenticity you don't find anywhere else. It is such a joy to touch people on a deep level. One can do that in India; in Europe and the USA it is difficult and rare.

This year I had to go to Canada for three months as my mother was dying. She had been to Auroville several times, and at the age of 84 seriously considered living here, but she couldn't get any suitable work and the ants got on her nerves, so she went back. She died without taking any drugs, while I read Sri Aurobindo and the Mother to her. It was unknown territory for both of us. I went through a period of guilt... should I have stayed in Ontario with her, should I have sacrificed these last few years to be with her? Eventually I felt I did the right thing in being here, as I didn't have the years left myself .

Having experienced the intensive care that a very old and sick person needs, I am now aware of how abysmally unprepared Auroville is for caring for the many old people that will need help in a few years. Right now there are about 150 people over 65 years of age, and this number will increase. We have little ground-level housing, no special taxi service, no nursing home. The young people will not be willing to care for us; it is not in their agenda or training. I always felt secure, that somehow I would be cared for here, but after seeing how intensive the care needed for my mother was, I was deeply shocked by the need it placed on the people around her. I am going to enquire into taking out extra insurance, though as I am now living on a maintanance I don't know if I can afford it. I definitely know I won't be able to go to the western style Apollo Hospital in Chennai as some people do. I strongly feel that some of us should get together and discuss the situation instead of just putting our heads in the sand.

My heart is very happy here, and I know I will die happily in Auroville.

Auralee passed away on 25th May 2022.

SANJEEV ... WHO CAME FROM DELHI IN 1981

When I was in college in Delhi in 1971 the political issues of India began to confront me, and I became acutely aware of the corruption and poverty of my country. After returning from a four month visit to Norway and England, where I saw a very different form of society, I felt very shaken up. I knew this awareness would be a driving force in my life from now on. I read everything I could get my hands on and did everything to experience different ways of being. I went to Ashrams in Rishikesh and travelled around looking at this India that was my home.

I had grown up in a middle class Delhi family and my father, grandfather and great-grandfather had been lawyers, so from day one that was my path and I had dutifully followed it. I worked at the profession for a while to save some money, but could not bear that way of life, and soon ran off. I studied philosophy, but when the money ran out I had to return to the Law. I felt as if I was floating like a ghost in the legal world; it really was not my cup of tea. I needed something more meaningful.

I was practising as a lawyer in 1981 and happened to be in Germany when a friend took me to see an exhibition on Auroville at the Max Müller Bhavan, which he thought I might find interesting. I was very impressed with what I saw there, and began to make contact with Sri Aurobindo and Auroville. This was the time of the conflict with the Sri Aurobindo Society, and after a while Auroville asked me if I would help them in my professional capacity. I said "Yes."

I worked with Kireet Joshi, an ex-Ashramite, drafting the legal letters, and he was a wonderful guide for me to Sri Aurobindo and the Mother. When Aurovilians were in Delhi I invited them to stay with me, and I used to chat for hours with them and got to know about Auroville first hand. I always have this faint recollection that, as a young boy of about 11, I visited Pondicherry with

Sanjeev

a large family group, and I may have seen the Mother; it is a dream-like recollection.

I visited Auroville a couple of times and became fascinated by it. I decided to take the jump. I had saved enough money to last me for two years, then after that everything would be a gamble. In October 1981 I packed my bags and came to Auroville.

Talking to Sanjeev after 26 years

I have now been here 26 years, and am continuously trying to find the meaning of this place and what I am doing here. It is a progressive effort, but the only realization I have come to is that one cannot understand what is happening here. The only way to function here is in an inner way, to try to silence the mind and seek direction from some other source. This process continues, and I expect it will continue for a long time.

It is as if Auroville is a field of growth for everyone, and yet different for each person. Also, there are always so many changes here, and people reflect that change. Sometimes you make a connection with a look, in a second ... it can happen.

On a collective and political level life can be very difficult here. It is a challenging field as it throws up many difficult issues. The line here between right and wrong is very fine. I have entered this field that I feel is very important, and in a way I like the challenges, but one can easily become battered by the constant head-on collisions. Most people do not enter this collective life, as they find the criticisms and the lack of remuneration difficult to take. One needs a very thick skin. It is much easier to be satisfied with one's own little nest, like in the outside world, but we need to challenge that presumption. Finance is not well organized here, and in the end everyone is left to fend for himself. People can only come and live here if they have money – or if they are desperate. We need young, competent people with families here to add to our richness of life. They need to be given a simple house and taken care of in a simple way. This has to be looked at, but it is as if the will to do so is not there. It is as if the older people here feel "we had it rough, so why can't they?" This is not a correct attitude. The leadership is hardly there nowadays; it has become very fragmented, as if many forces are pulling many ways. I feel the centralized planning is also weak, as individual projects have become more important than community ones. Often our rules are not clear and that causes a lot of confusion and aggravation.

I personally feel very blessed. I work with SAIIER (Sri Aurobindo International Institute of Educational Research), which covers many aspects of Auroville. In my own life I am part of the Auroville level, the SAIIER level, and I have a connection with Udavi School and an interaction with my family. We now live in a new house behind the new Pour Tous, and in our family there are four of us, who come from Ethiopia, Germany, North India and Tamil Nadu, a challenge of nationalities right here in our own house. When I came here at first it was a great blow for my own North Indian family, as I was the eldest son, with many expectations. I had been groomed for the family profession, and my parents were in tears for a long time. They slowly adjusted when they came and visited me and saw how happy I was here.

I think I have got the most satisfaction here from my involvement with Udavi School, as I like children. It was a challenge to try out new ideas and collect a good team, and I believe we have created something special there. My involvement with the Kindergarten has also given me a lot of satisfaction.

The real Auroville is an inner movement; the line where it begins is very subtle. We are a very privileged lot to be here. It is a secret paradise that is not easily visible.

GRACE ... WHO CAME FROM GANDIGRAM, NEAR MADURAI, IN SOUTH INDIA IN 1987

I was born in 1965 and had one brother, but our parents died when we were six so we were placed in Gandhigram Orphanage. Before that I don't know where I was. There were about two hundred and fifty children staying there aged one month to eighteen years and I lived there very happily for fifteen years. I still go back and visit "my family" as I think of them, whenever I can. The only problem was with the food; there was very little of it as the Government grant was not large enough to feed everyone well. Friends collected money and food to help us, but I was very thin and I remember I was allowed to have one egg a week because they were worried about me, instead of the official half an egg a week.

I used to walk the four kilometres each way to the school, but when I was fifteen I wanted to go to work so I could get some money and have nice sarees like the girls in the town. I got a job in a hospital which paid me twenty rupees a month, as I had board and food free. I was so happy with the food there; curd, milk, and as many vegetables as I wanted. I was the youngest person there, and I remember how the other girls would go back to their families at holiday time, but I stayed on and worked as I had no family to go to.

One day Saraswatidevi, a social worker, came to the hospital and we became friendly. She told me about Auroville, what a beautiful place it was, how nice the foreigners were, and why didn't I come with her to see for myself. I was immediately attracted to the idea and told the hospital matron I would like to go, but she said that if I did, and there were any problems, she didn't want me back. This shocked me, but I decided to go, and in 1985 I came to Auroville. I was surprised by the tall trees and all the foreigners with white skins and the Indians who looked like foreigners in their western clothes and who spoke good English. The food was very good with lots of bread.

They put me in Last School and I stayed in a keet hut at Bliss community. I felt terribly alone, although I was sharing it with two other girls. I was afraid of the blackness as we only had candles; there was a lamp, but it was "only for emergencies." I was also afraid of the snakes and that huge space everywhere. I had lived all my life with many people around me in the orphanage and in the hospital, and now here I was, living in the middle of nowhere. I also didn't speak any English so I felt completely isolated. After five months of crying every night I decided to go back to the hospital and face the matron's anger. She shouted at me, but did take me back as I had been a good worker, and I stayed there for the next two years. In the evenings I went to a typing class which I thought would help me in my future.

Then I met Nagappan, a quiet and caring man, and we got married. He had grown up in Auroville and wanted to take me back there with him. He was living and working at the Matrimandir and got fifty rupees a month, so when we got married we stayed in his brother's house in Kottakarai. It was awful there as the rain came in and it was full of mosquitos. I had always lived in a town, and didn't know how to collect firewood and make a fire and how to cook. I was frightened of the cows and dogs. I didn't like to take a bath as the bathroom was open and I thought men would look in. The dialect was different

Grace

and people used words I didn't know. Everything was very different and very difficult. After a while we got our own capsule house at the Pump House, but that was a difficult place to live in as there were no doors or windows and the village children used to climb in and steal the pots. I remember cooking with my husband holding an umbrella over me, and then emptying the pot with the rice and starting to make the sambal in the same pot as we only had one pot. Each month when he got his salary we would buy one spoon or some small thing. For two years we had a very hard time.

In 1988 I went to the Entry Group and applied to become an Aurovilian. I had been told to learn a few sentences to say about Mother and why I wanted to come here, but my only reason was to get a house and a job. Somehow I did become an Aurovilian and got a job as the storekeeper at Auromode for sixteen rupees a day and we were able to buy milk and eggs so things improved.

One day a Dutch lady called Mauna asked me if I would like a job as a typist at Matrimandir. I didn't quite understand what she was saying, so I just said, "Yes, yes, yes!" Mauna encouraged me by giving me English books, and when my first child was born prematurely she helped me a lot. In 1990 Matrimandir got the first computer and somehow I learned to use it, even though I still knew very little English.

It was only when I had a proper job and felt I could contribute something that I finally felt I had become an Aurovilian. It had been a long struggle.

Talking to Grace after 21 years

I came here in 1987. I loved my husband and I loved Auroville. The only real problems were money, as we didn't have any, and language, as I didn't know any English. In those days there were no English classes, so Mauna got me some books from Madras and used to push me to learn English. When you don't know a language you cannot express your emotions. People think you are stupid, as if "you have no brain." It took me a long time to have the courage to ask if I didn't understand what someone was saying to me. These two things, money and language, are big problems for Tamil people. The worst thing that ever happened to me was when my son, Arun, was born one month prematurely and I was rushed to Jipmer hospital. As I had no family here and my mother in law was very old, there was nobody to give me food in the hospital. For three days I had no tea or food and was terribly hungry and depressed. Eventually Hilde from Auroville came to see me, and I stayed in Centre Field for one month till I recovered. If we have no family in our tradition things can be difficult.

My husband is a quiet man and so I found friends through my work. I have always loved my work and it has been very important to me. I work at Matrimandir, and as my service clean and do the flowers every morning at Savitri Bhavan. I feel attracted to Mother through Shraddhavan, who I think is a wonderful woman.

Four years ago the Women's Group was started and this changed my life. I asked Bindu and two German women who were interested in the women's movement how to set up a group. We didn't know what to do at first, so started a singing group which they loved. We now have about 60 women in the group, which has spilt into two different groups, the Mirra group and the Collaboration group. It has been and still is difficult for everyone, as we have never done anything like this before. The women feel as if they are at school and everyone wants to be boss. We have all had to learn how to run a meeting and listen to each other. Every time I have to say to them, "Be on time; be responsible;" I say this to them every month. We have a few rules, like not being personal about things, which is very difficult for them as many of the women are often related and family issues easily come up. And being punctual, like four o'clock means four o'clock. And to give 25 rupees a month. We are now able to give small loans up to 2,000 rupees with no interest, and we take the money from their Pour Tous account. We don't charge interest, as Mother said that money should not be used for making money, so this must apply to even our very small amounts. It is difficult for me to raise money as my English is not good and I have no contacts in France or Germany like other groups in Auroville. I don't know many foreigners here, I don't know how to ask for money, and there is nobody to guide us. I was terribly nervous to approach Sanjeev for a grant from SAIIER, but now they do help. We were advised to make handicrafts and cakes and have a fair and sell them, and we did this. We have now done this five times, but not made any money, which is disappointing.

The Women's Sports Day is a big annual event and gets bigger and better each year, but it takes a lot of money and organization. So does organizing our classes for tailoring, basket making, singing and painting. It gives the women a huge amount of confidence to do these little things in a group. They have never done anything like this before. It is a big step for them.

My dreams? One day to go back and serve in the hospital where I used to work. In 1989 I made good friends with an American woman, and I hope one day to maybe see her again, or even visit her. Also that the villages develop economically, as I see there are still a lot of poor people living there, especially women. These are my main big dreams.

> **The Mother**
>
> ...this fact is so obvious that a simple and ignorant peasant here is, in his heart, closer to the Divine than the intellectuals of Europe. All those who want to become Aurovilians must know this and behave accordingly; otherwise they are unworthy of being Aurovilians.
>
> Those who are in contact with the villagers should not forget that these people are worth as much as they are, that they know as much, that they think and feel as well as they do. They should therefore never have an attitude of ridiculous superiority. They are at home and you are the visitor.

BANU ... WHO CAME FROM VILLUPURAM, SOUTH INDIA, IN 1987

I was born in Valavanur, a small town outside Pondicherry, in 1963, and had three sisters and a very happy family life. My father and grandfather had been tobacco merchants and we were always well off and secure. Then when I was in 10th standard my father became sick and spent one year in hospital, then died there. I will never forget that journey at 4 am on the bus to tell my grandfather he had died. It was my first bus journey alone, and it was like the end of the world.

We had to go and live with my grandmother, and it was a disaster. She treated us like servants, and it got so bad that the four of us ran away one night. I was fourteen and my sisters were younger and life became a nightmare. I couldn't go to school as we had no money, so I worked in a fancy shop selling bangles. I used to work from eight till ten at night for one hundred rupees a month, on which we had to live. My mother was a vegetable selling lady in the market on a Sunday, and somehow we managed. We also had a little job arranging matchsticks in a frame for ten paisa a frame. I think my mother suffered a lot as she saw how her daughters had to live in those years.

I couldn't bear to spend the rest of my life living like that, just working and worrying, so I somehow managed to save enough money to go to college to study accountancy. Friends helped me, and in two years I had passed my B.A. Economics.

I was never an excellent student, despite my ambition, as I had very high spirits and loved to do dancing and go in fancy dress competitions and had lots of friends. My grandfather helped to pay the college fees, though I remember mine were always paid last, which humiliated me. He also threatened me that if I failed even one subject he would have me thrown out. It was all very difficult, as it was an English medium school and I only knew Tamil, so I had a double burden. Friends helped me to buy clothes and things like soap and combs, but I had no money for the bus fare and had to walk the four kilometres each way to the college.

In 1985 I finished college, and one day a friend asked me if I would like to visit this strange place called Auroville with her. I was up for anything, ready to see the world and start my new career, so I said a big "Yes" to her. It was the first time I had ever seen white people! I wanted to touch them, to see what their skin felt like.

I saw how people were living together, rich and poor, there was no difference; I couldn't believe it. I desperately wanted to be there with them. I needed to be with people, as by then I was completely alone in the world. I made enquiries about coming there, and on May 27th, 1987 – I will never, never forget the date – I came to see about a job in Auroville. I remember a large Italian typing machine that I had one week's training on. They seemed satisfied with me, and I started work for three hundred rupees a month. I was so proud!

I got a job in the Technical Trust and lived in New Creation for two years, where I met my future husband, Vengadesh.

Banu

I will never forget my first dawn bonfire that happened just after I arrived in Auroville. I was the first person there! I just couldn't believe this had happened to me. Mother had taken me under Her wing.

Talking with Banu after 22 years

It is now 2008, and I find it difficult to believe that I am now living in Portsmouth in the south west of England. My husband, Vengadesh, by the miracle of an English friend's hard work, was able to join the British Royal Navy, and is now a steward on a troop ship that carries 2,000 crew, which is almost the same population as Auroville.

My two daughters are aged 8 and 11, we have been here a year now, and we have a nice house on a naval estate. Life here is very different from Atithi Griha Guest House in Auroville, and from Pondicherry where my mother and two sisters live. I was the manager of the Guest House for five years, and felt very proud of my job, as I was the only Tamil manager of a guest house in Auroville, and a woman also.

At first here I found freedom from Indian family responsibility good, but then the other side of that is the feeling of isolation when people stick to their own little houses. Everybody gets into their cars in the morning to go to work, and then they keep the doors and windows closed, as it is cold and they are frightened of robbers. Even in the summer children don't play in the street, as the parents are afraid for them. It is very difficult to make friends here. My English is not very good, and this makes me feel uncomfortable sometimes. I listen to the TV and try and improve my English; in fact I watch a lot of TV. Also in this area there are very few Indian people, never mind Tamil people. In England most of the Indians live in London or the north. I have found one shop in Portsmouth town that sells the spices I want, and once they even had snake gourd vegetable.

At first I found it very cold, even in the English summer. The winters are cold and grey, and last from October to March. During the winter it gets dark at 4.30 in the afternoon. English people are very quiet and orderly; nobody pushes or shoves or shouts or fights. Nobody walks on the roads or throws rubbish down. If the police see you throwing rubbish they can make you pay a £50 fine (approx Rs.3,800). All the cows live in their fields, and the dogs live in houses. Sometimes I even see dogs riding in cars.

My two daughters are very happy here and go skating and hiking with their friends. I am proud when their teacher tells me they have the best writing in the school, and they get very high marks in everything. They are much more disciplined and hard working than the English children. I think they will have a good future here.

My main problem is getting a good job. Because my English is not so good it is difficult. I am trying to get up the courage to go to a college and improve my accountancy skills, but I haven't yet got around to it. I am still trying to coordinate my daughter's needs with my own. Vengadesh is away for weeks at a time on his ship and so it is difficult to plan things. He tells me I will have to begin with a lowly job to get experience, but I don't really like that.

This is a wonderful challenge to live here. I never thought it would happen to me.

* * * * *

Jayashree, Banu's 11 year old daughter, giggles at her first impression of England. "I couldn't believe the houses had glass windows and no netting. And there are carpets in all the rooms except the kitchen. Nothing bites you here. If English people see one fly or spider in their house they go crazy and spray it to death. I wondered where everyone was when we first came, as the streets were empty as the people stay indoors watching TV, then get into their cars. Everyone has a car here, except us. I want a cat or a dog like all my friends have, but Dad says no, he doesn't want them in the house. My friend's dog, Spotty, even sleeps on her bed.

I really love being here, and the only thing I miss really is our Indian family. The schools are much better, as the teachers are friendly and relaxed, and don't try to scare you. (Do you know, some Indian schools have a "stick lady!") At break we are only allowed fruit and not chocolate or biscuits, and every day we have a different lunch, and on Tuesdays we have Chinese. I love to go ice-skating with my friend Emma on Saturday morning, and afterwards we have chips and a milk shake. I like going to her house as her parents are very kind to each other and look after their pets very well and give them good food. I love going to Asda supermarket and looking at their 'George' clothes – they are really cool. In winter you need different clothes so we have to do lots of clothes shopping. The streets are very clean here and everyone walks on the pavement, not all over the road like they do in India. English people are very clean and quiet. I like that. I can walk out on my own here; it feels safe."

GUY ... WHO CAME FROM BELGIUM IN 1988

I was born the day my home town was liberated from German occupation. I have often thought of the agonies my mother must have endured when she was carrying me in her womb, sleeping in bunkers during the bombardments and trying to stay alive during the liberation fight. Her fears must have made a great impact on me, creating a deep sense of insecurity. Looking back, I can see how these feelings didn't make it easy for me to jump into the Auroville adventure. Indeed, after my first visit in 1973, it took me fifteen years to finally join the community.

I was the youngest of six children, and somehow always in the way of my older brothers. I always felt I was disturbing them and so learned to keep a distance. My deep involvement with sports saved me as a teenager. Then suddenly I was thrown out of my school for challenging authority, and my life changed abruptly. My new school had no sports programme, and I began to become alienated from friends and the life I had known so far. I went to study economics, my father's choice, at university, but after a couple of years I dropped out dissatisfied.

Then began a strange period of hibernation. I shut myself up in my room overlooking the wide open fields of Flanders, listening to music, and reading one book after the other. I felt something coming up within me, but I did not know what or how to deal with it. Eventually my parents made me get a job and I started working at a university library. After a few years, I married and moved to Antwerp, which was a new life. I worked in a bookshop and publishing house, met authors and open-minded people, and life began to open up. But a deep yearning for something else was always present.

One day in 1970 my life changed. I was thumbing through a copy of "Bres Planate", a French publication in Dutch, a sort of new age magazine, and came across an article which called an Indian man the "Teilhard de Chardin of the

East". The first page showed a photograph of a beautiful young face with shining eyes looking into the future. I thought instantly, "This man knows." A few months later the magazine published an article on Auroville, and I knew I had to go.

With Mother's permission, my wife and I came to live in Auroville in September 1973. Sadly enough, it turned out to be an overwhelming struggle of fear and insecurities. We decided to return to Belgium after three months. On the last day, I went to sit at the Samadhi, full of agitation and indecision about my future. Suddenly, a solid block of Light descended into me and filled me with a wonderful sense of peace and a quiet mind. This 'state of grace' stayed with me for months. After our return to Belgium, by some miracle, my wife and I got our old jobs back and we found a nice place to live. There we were, in exactly the same situation as before we left, yet everything had changed and felt different.

After five years I came back to Auroville for a visit, alone this time, and realized why I had not been ready before. I was not yet ready to give up my job and my secure way of life. I was stuck in my attachments, and I knew that stepping out into insecurity would be very difficult. Altogether it took me another ten years. In between I visited Auroville every two years, with a growing yearning to live here.

Finally, in 1988, I arrived with my new partner. From the first day I felt completely at home. I knew I had come at the right time. Unfortunately, although we had visited Auroville together two years before and she was eager to live in Auroville, circumstances turned out to be extremely difficult for my partner. She was not able to connect with Auroville's inner and outer reality, and returned to Belgium after two and a half years. Going back with her would have been an inner suicide for me.

After all those years, I had finally "come home". I have felt like this till today.

Talking to Guy after 20 years

My Newcomer period was a time of grace. And I still feel after 20 years that Auroville is my home and my place for the rest of my life.

For 15 years I worked in the office of the Auroville Centre for Scientific Research (CSR). I was also secretary-coordinator of the Auroville Project Coordination Group for almost 19 years. I found this extremely interesting work, and enjoyed being a link between the community and two foundations which annually support Auroville projects: the Foundation for World Education in the USA and Stichting De Zaaier in The Netherlands. It was enriching to see the dreams of fellow Aurovilians. I appreciated how they tried to manifest their projects in farming, reforestation, health, education and in other areas. I always felt a Force, that is the only word I can use, behind their work, and it felt so worthwhile and indeed a privilege to be of some help in this.

Between 1997 and 2006, I was also strongly involved with the "Land for Auroville" project. The first years were greatly rewarding, and sustained me to face the challenge of securing the remaining land for Auroville. Unfortunately, when the purchase process was suspended in 2003 for almost three years, my energies became blocked. I hung on trying to find solutions, but not much could be done. This difficult situation, however, led to a significant change in my life in Auroville.

For almost 20 years I had attended countless meetings and discussions, and now I wanted to step back and have some quiet time for myself. As my involvement with the land had come to a natural ending, I decided to take a one-year "sabbatical". (In the university world a "sabbatical" is given to professors every seven years so they can pursue their own reading and research without the pressures of daily work.) It took me a long time to wrap up and hand over my different jobs. In the beginning I discovered how much personal identification I had put into my work, and actually how difficult it was to give it up. I was also concerned as to what people within the community would think, how they would react, and I began making all sorts of ridiculous projections. Another concern was, "What about my karma yoga and my commitment towards the community?" On the other hand, I could not deny the strong impulse from within to take this step.

I finally discontinued my work towards the end of 2006, and although at first I thought my work mates might be disapproving, they turned out to be sympathetic. Also many other Aurovilian friends encouraged me and supported me in my decision. This is a wonderful thing about Auroville, that you have the opportunity and the space to do what you sincerely need.

Meanwhile I had discovered the wonders of water therapy at Quiet. I had some remarkably beautiful experiences receiving a Watsu, a warm water therapy, and decided to learn it myself. I took a number of courses and practiced as much as I could. And now that my sabbatical is over I give sessions at the Quiet Healing Centre. In my experience, the water and the silent support by the therapist is an extremely simple but effective way to let go and reach a deep level of inner peace. The work transcends words. When I give a session I feel it is as beneficial as receiving one. I go into a quiet inner state, like in a meditation, and sink into deep layers of peace. And below that space I often feel a whole layer of Love, that deep sense of connectedness and universal love that is always there within us. What a wonderful work!

The icing on the cake is my partner Anandi. We have been together very happily for 15 years now. She is an urban Tamil lady who has the perfect combination of the deep spiritual life of ancient India and a very modern dynamic approach to life. She runs KOFPU, the Kottakarai Organic Food Production Unit, with a passion and energy that it is always a joy to see.

Yes, Mother has taken extremely good care of me in Auroville.

Guy

MAHALINGAM ... WHO CAME FROM SOUTH INDIA IN 1988

I was born in about 1920, though my parents were not sure of the exact year, in a little Tamil village. My father was a small merchant and was illiterate, as were most village people in those days. I was sent to the local Christian school, and although my parents were Hindus it didn't matter to them because at that time Christian schools were the only ones available. They had no apprehension that I might be influenced by their religious teachings; I don't think it ever occurred to them. Caste meant much more to them than being a Christian.

My father sent me to college, and I was the first Hindu boy in all our local villages to attend college. I studied maths, physics and chemistry and loved learning, but in my intermediate year I mixed with boys who were not serious, and we used to go to the cinema and fool about and I failed my exams.

When the Second World War broke out I decided to join the army, and went off without telling my parents. I was so naive; I didn't realize the army would pay you, and that I could have been trained as an officer, so I just signed on and became a sepoy. I thought I would be sent to Europe and have adventures, but it was nothing like that, and after a short time I quit. Nationalist feelings were running strong in India, and Nehru had been jailed for seven years for making anti-war speeches, and I didn't want to be part of the war movement.

I joined a training school for teachers and enjoyed it, and have taught ever since. Then I came upon Vivekananda's books and my life changed. I read his nine volumes and all the available Ramakrishna and Vivekananda literature. I was very attracted to Ramakrishna, and felt a new world opening up for me as I immersed myself in their works. I wanted to join the Ramakrishna Mutt, and wrote to ask them if I could join them. When they wrote back asking if I was a graduate, with the arrogance of youth I said to myself that Ramakrishna himself was not well educated and so I didn't reply to their letter .

I read Swami Shivananda's book on yoga and wrote to him to ask if I could be his disciple. I wanted to have a living guru as I was tired of just reading books. I went to his ashram in Rishikesh but quickly realized that it was not my place, I didn't feel good there. It was as if something inside myself was saying "go away, go away ", and after two weeks I left.

I came back to Tirunelvela and continued my studies, but I wasn't quite sure what to do with myself. One day, on the last day of our exams, I met a friend whom I had not seen for a long time. He gave me a copy of the Tamil translation of Mother's "Conversations", as he knew I was interested in that sort of thing and he didn't know anyone else to give the book to. I never met him again, but my life was changed. I found the Tamil translations of Sri Aurobindo's "Basis of Yoga" and "The Mother" and was transfixed. I read in a newspaper article that Sri Aurobindo gave darshan four times a year, and I wrote to the Ashram asking permission to go to the darshan. Four times I wrote and four times they replied saying that this was not the right time.

I eventually got permission to attend and excitedly rushed off to Pondicherry. I felt a great longing to join the Ashram and wrote asking if I could join them, but again the answer was "Not now." In 1955 I came for darshan, and out of the blue M.P. Pandit asked me if I would like to join? I was overjoyed after all that waiting, but only stayed for three years. My friends used to call me a rolling stone because they felt I could never stick to anything, but the reason for leaving was that my father was old and I was the only earning member of the family. That was the "outward reason"; I am not sure of the "inward" reason. I remember someone saying to the Mother that I was always coming and going, and she turned to them and said: "How do you know his destiny?" I stayed supporting my family for two years, but was very unhappy in the outside world. Once, when I had left, Mother asked the Ashram manager why I wanted to go away, and he told her of my family's financial difficulties. She asked him how much I was giving them a month, and he told her fifty rupees. She arranged for the Ashram to send them sixty rupees a month! That is how Mother did things.

Mother took me back into the Ashram and again I left. This happened three times, and each time she took me back. Somehow I couldn't fit in with the Ashram life. I felt Mother and Sri Aurobindo were not just human beings – they were much, much more than that. I wanted to be near them, but actually living there never worked out for me. I really think it was because I didn't feel worthy to be there, as I was so attached to my family .

When I retired from my work as a teacher years later, I came back to the Ashram again and worked in the gardens.

Mahalingam

Then one day something very strange happened. A conference was being held in the Ashram and a German man called Michel Klosterman was sitting in the hall waiting for the meeting to start. He told me later that when I entered the room and he saw me, he heard a voice saying; "Take him to Auroville." When he told me this I immediately said, "Yes, yes, I will go to Auroville". I was very happy there, but then the troubles between the Sri Aurobindo Society and some people in Auroville started, and I felt very uncomfortable and sad about it, so decided to leave Auroville.

I went back to my village and sold Ashram books for VAK. I was very friendly with Joss at Pitchandikulam and told him that I would like to return and live in Auroville again, and he promised to try and find a place for me. Then I had a very strange dream. I dreamt I was in a forest space in an area about the size of a tennis court and in one corner Mother was taking a class. Someone told me Mother was calling me, and when I looked Mother stood up and came over to me and said, "Here is Mahalingam." I was overwhelmed and touched her feet in pranam.

The very next day I received a letter from Joss telling me to come to Auroville and that he had found a place for me to live.

Through Mother's help I continue to be here. My soul is connected to her and she won't let me leave. She is a sun towards which I am drawn.

Talking with Mahalingam after 21 years

Although I am now 88 years old, most of the time I feel like a forty-year-old. I love walking on Auroville's tree-lined roads, and every day walk about 8 or 9 kilometres. I live in Fraternity in a little group of houses that is like a small Tamil village, so I am not isolated, and people help me with shopping if I need it. I have organised myself to take the Auroville buses into Pondicherry twice a week, where I visit the Ashram and the Samadhi, and a bus picks me up to go to Transformation School, where I sit in a quiet corner and work on my translations.

This has always been my outer work. I find it impossible to meditate, even for half an hour, so I do the translating with a feeling of dedication and aspiration, and this seems to be my way. I have translated 15 volumes of "Mother's Collected Works" into Tamil, and this is my sadhana. In the evenings I sit in front of photos of Mother and Sri Aurobindo, and this is the time I often feel that I am not this body but quite something else.

Recently I have found my aspiration has once again intensified, as it was in my early years. I am grateful to Mother that she has kept me free of outer desires or wants. I live very simply in my little house in the trees and am free to pursue my outer and inner life as I wish. I am a very contented man.

BOB ... WHO CAME FROM ENGLAND IN 1988

When I was 12 years old I was confirmed into the Church of England and had a very strong feeling that I wanted to give my life to God, that this seemed to be the only worthwhile aim in life. Attending the Confirmation classes had awoken something in me, as I had never had the opportunity to talk with anyone about these things before. I thought I might like to be a priest, but vaguely felt, even at that age, that that sort of life would never be broad or wide enough for me. Around that age I started doing massage on people, and very often they got a lot better. I never knew why until I meet Jean, my second wife, many years later, and she explained what was really happening.

I became an engineer, which has always stood me in good stead, then years later, when I was employed as a social worker, I met Jean, who introduced me to Sri Aurobindo's yoga and to Auroville. After that I also attended Marguerite Smithwhite's meditation classes in London. There I continued to learn about Auroville and was captivated by the concept of this international city based on Sri Aurobindo's philosophy.

In 1980 I brought my first wife and two children to Auroville and worked on the Matrimandir. I remember when the plane landed at Bombay and I came out into the thick pea soup humid Indian air, I just wanted to collapse on the ground saying "I've come home, I've come home." I never recognized before that I had not felt at home anywhere else. Conditions in Auroville in those days were quite harsh, and my wife was terrified of scorpions and snakes and "poochies" in general. There was no school for the children, and I set up some classes in Ami, but everything was chaotic. After three months we returned to England, but I knew I would return. I returned later that year, again working on Matrimandir and in the workshop.

My wife and I later divorced, and my life changed drastically. Now I wanted simplicity and a sense of purpose in my life; I only wanted what I could carry in one rucksack. In Auroville, I developed a serious case of hepatitis which gave me an enforced period of rest, and I read the "The Life Divine". The world of Indian philosophy was a revelation to me.

Meeting Jean, who later became my second wife, transformed my life, as she was involved in spiritual healing and understood many things of which I was only half aware. We decided we wanted to go and live permanently in Auroville, but we realised we needed some capital, so we went to work in Saudi Arabia. In some ways it was a strange life, as we lived with the British ex-pats, with whom we had little in common, and with Saudi people, whose society was impossible to access. Life there was difficult for foreign women, and the children would throw stones at Jean as they believed that Western women were loose and immoral.

I remember working in a large office in Riyadh after the Gulf War ended. I would go early to the office in the morning and do my yoga asanas and meditation before anyone came in. I began to notice that on the days I did not do this, the atmosphere in the office was always less peaceful. It was as if the little effort I had made affected the day's energies, and everyone was touched by it. I realised that this was how I could be of help: by working in a quiet, occult way I could help to raise the level of conciousness.

Jean and I loved to go camping in the desert and spending nights under the huge desert skies. The peace was tangible out there, and gave us the strength for our daily challenges of living in that rather artificial environment.

We came to Auroville after six years of working in Saudi Arabia, built our house down on the beach at Sri Ma, and felt that we were doing that which we were being asked to do.

Talking with Bob after 8 years

In 2006, after eight very happy years of living in Auroville, Jean's health began to suffer with the heat and humidity. We installed air conditioning in two of our rooms, but it didn't help, so our only choice was to return to England. We had kept in close contact with our family in England and Canada, visiting them every year, and now it is good to be near our grandchildren and to be able to be of help to them.

The main problem, as it is for many returning Aurovilians, is money. House prices in England are now very high, and as we had no property to sell we were in a difficult situation. Fortunately my brother lent us money for a house, which was extremely generous of him, as he knows he will not get it back for a long time.

We are now in our early seventies with no savings and only a small pension, so I am trying to build up my healing practice. This is proving unsatisfactory as I am not registered with the authorities, and our little house is too small to work privately at home. Fortunately I am doing renovation work on buildings so am occupied and earning some money. I find it strange to take money for work after those years of living in Auroville and working for the Divine and being taken care of by the Divine. But here one has to pay the bills and be involved in the British way of life. Many aspects of urban civilisation are quite wonderful, however. The buses stop across the road, and I have a free 'senior citizen' bus pass – no more being rattled to death on Indian roads. The beds are soft, the water hot, and things work. Communication is blissfully easy, as everyone speaks English and the shared humour oils relationships. Being near our family and grandchildren is a joy. Jean's health has improved somewhat, though she still has difficulties; but then nowhere is perfect. We miss Auroville terribly.

We are still very involved with Auroville, and meet old friends at meetings and at people's houses all over the country. We avidly read "Auroville Today" when it drops through the letter box, and feel a very strong psychic connection that links our daily lives with Auroville.

On that level it doesn't really matter where you live, the Divine is everywhere.

Bob and Jean

Jean ... Bob's wife.

My parents were committed Christians and were determined I would not grow up as a "heathen", as they delicately put it, so I was sent to all the Church services and Sunday Schools possible. In my early teens, however, I recognized that I could no longer stand up in church and say the Creed or accept all the doctrine. I stopped going, and for years my father was terribly upset and it caused us both a lot of pain.

For the next few years I was buzzing with questions and read voraciously, but I could not find satisfactory answers. One evening when I was in my early twenties I happened to turn on the TV and saw "Meeting Point", a religious half hour programme irreverently called "the God-slot". The speakers were Judge Christmas Humphries, the foremost Buddhist in Britain at the time, Marghanita Laski, a humanist, and a beautiful Indian man called Arabinda Basu. He was a revelation to me. I had never seen or heard anyone like him; I felt he was talking directly to me. I immediately wrote to him via the BBC, and a week later I received a letter from him asking me if I would like to have tea with him when next he was in London.

We met at Margaret Fletcher's house, near the Victoria and Albert Museum, and we talked for hours. I told him I had always been clairvoyant and that for a couple of years I had been visited, on a subtle level, by a small, dark complexioned, grey bearded man who taught me to meditate. I had no idea who he was. When I described this old gentleman to my host he excused himself for a couple of minutes then came back into the room carrying a photograph. "Is this the old gentleman who has been teaching you? His name is Sri Aurobindo." (He had been dead for three years by then). This was my introduction to Sri Aurobindo, the Mother, and the yoga.

Mother had told Arabinda to take a teaching post at Durham University, and he remained there for 14 years. He invited me to stay with his family, and arranged access for me to the Gulbenkian Museum of Oriental Art and the University Library. I devoured everything I could in this new world, and under his guidance began my education into the spiritual life of India. I used to visit the Sri Aurobindo Centre in Bell Street in London, and it was there that I met Shraddhavan and Judith, who were staying there at that time, sleeping on the floor in the meditation room.

I was eventually able to visit India in 1974. The journey was chaotic as the plane was late and I missed my connections and arrived in Pondicherry in the middle of the night. The dark streets seemed to be crowded with people sleeping on the pavements, and I didn't know what to do, except just lie down beside them outside the Ashram and wait till dawn. As I was settling down and trying to protect my luggage, a young Indian man dressed in white came cycling down the road and waved at me. "Hello, I am Mohan," he said. "Mother has awoken me and told me one of her children has arrived in Pondicherry. 'You must go and bring her to stay with you,' she told me, so here I am. Please come with me." So I followed him to his tiny flat on Aurobindo Street and slept in his bed while he slept on a mat on the floor by my side. This was my introduction to the Ashram. Mohan has remained part of my spiritual family since then.

Many years later I was able, with Bob, to return to Auroville and begin a new life.

Jean Neal passed away on 10th July 2020.

HOLGER ... WHO CAME FROM GERMANY IN 1990

I grew up with a mother who was often doing asanas, sitting cross-legged on the floor or stretching and bending, as she suffered from a bad back and that was the only thing that helped her. When I was about fourteen my parents travelled to Russia, Mexico and India, and as a teenager I thought this was really "cool", thought India was definitely the "coolest."

I remember reading a small article in a newspaper about a place in South India called Auroville, and I thought: "What a good idea; that is how society should go." I was not very fond of socializing and parties, so I used to meet a friend regularly to discuss "How we can define the rules of an alternative society." We decided it had to be based on completely different grounds from the society we saw around us, but we always came up against one major insoluble problem. That was how it should deal with the people who did not want to work. He said;"Expel them." I said, "Then there is no point in starting the project." Our debates came to an end after we once spent a whole night walking through the streets of Munich discussing this insurmountable problem. We never saw each other again.

I became politically active, but after a few years began to see how a political solution for the planet was impossible. So I turned to psychology, especially the theories of Wilhelm Reich, and I got married to a psychologist. I read psychological books, undertook psychotherapy, and tried to understand my inner world. Although this was partly successful, it was incomplete.

In retrospect this search was leading me logically towards a spirituality question. Therefore I made contact with a Sufi teacher from Egypt and entered the classical Sufi path. But the man died under mysterious circumstances and made me turn away from this line of spirituality. A bit later I found an Indian guru and continued to meditate under his guidance. At this time I had finished my studies at the Music University of Salzburg, and worked as nurse in a mental hospital.

On completion of my social service, I finally went to India. I didn't want to go as a tourist so I said to myself I would stay in every place I found myself for at least one week, to really value the atmosphere of the place. That was good for me as it made me concentrate and slow down my perception of time. I also went to visit the guru who had initiated me in Puri, and I was very disappointed when he didn't seem to recognize me. This really hit my pride, and I sat in my room for three days, scribbling in my diary. When the hurt ego quietened down I observed that I had come on this spiritual path for all the wrong reasons. I decided to cut my Indian trip short, go back to Germany and build a career in music and not touch any of these matters till I was thirty, when I would hopefully be mature enough.

I successfully immersed myself in my career. On my thirtieth birthday I was sitting with my drinking colleagues after a concert. I weighed eighty four kilos and drank every night. And I did not intend to pick up the path.

Some time before, I had met Tina. We were both divorced; I was working hard on my musical career; she had two children to care for. Yet we were both unfulfilled.

Tina, however, had little knowledge about spirituality. At least I knew what I was missing out on as I had looked into some alternatives, and my music kept me frantically busy. I gave her my old spiritual books to read, and she quickly turned out to be the more dynamic part in our relationship. We went to La Palma to see a friend who was doing yoga, and Tina's interest was stimulated even more. "Have you heard of Auroville?" she asked me on our return. I smiled knowingly ."I almost went there on my trip to India." The next day she presented me with five plane tickets to Chennai, and we left for a two month trip with two small children and a young baby, our first son.

This was 1990, and life in Auroville could be quite tough. And it was tough for us as a couple also. I felt Tina admired my experience of life, which of course was 95% her projection, and very quickly vanished in Auroville. I was knocked down from my high horse, as expected. Yet, it was painful. Especially as I had just separated from the string quartet I had been with for six years in Germany; we must have given nearly 1,000 concerts together and the split was unsettling for me. I felt I had lost the quality of my life, and without a career in music I felt I would be a nobody. Tina wanted to move to Auroville immediately but I told her; "We are not yet ready for it. Aurovilians are much more advanced than us, we need more spiritual experience. (I don't know where I got this idea. We had met lots of really nice people there; but were the 'advanced' Aurovilians hiding in the bushes?) I think it will take us three years to prepare ourselves."

To find a new anchor in my musical life, I went to Calcutta to study Indian music. On Xmas day I rang Tina to wish her Happy Christmas. The line was crackling and we had to shout at each other. She told me she was pregnant and wanted the baby to be born in Auroville, and that she was packing right now as it was the cool time of the year, the right time to go and get settled. "Slow down, what about my things?", I shouted. "I am not packing your things, just mine; you will have to decide for yourself," she said. The family of my music teacher was a very traditional Muslim family with four gifted and dutiful sons and a mother who used to bring them food, while they were caring for the music alone. You can imagine how utterly incomprehensible my situation was to them.

But I went back to Germany, and in three weeks we had sold everything and were on a plane to Auroville. That is how I came here.

Talking with Holger after 19 years

The other day someone asked the Dalai Lama, "What are you?" and he answered, "I am a monk." He knows he is much more that that of course, but when I heard that answer I realized, "Oh, yes, I am a musician." Sometimes I ask myself if I need this identity, but then I see it as being on a small level of something greater. I recently saw an interview with probably the world's greatest guitarist, and I felt so close to him, as if we were part of the same world, and that was nice.

I don't have as many needs on a vital level as I did when I was 25. Music is nowadays a means of inner development, a tool by which I grow, as are many other things. I guess Auroville is a tool in that sense. Also now I feel I belong to certain things, like my wife Tina and my family and Auroville, and I would not go away or leave them; we just belong together.

I have been here 19 years now and could write a book about it. At first I found things difficult as I had lost my identity of being a musician. I was willing to forego that as I had a vague impression that it could be a hindrance to my development, but it caused a few painful years. I did some compositions, but it was as if they belonged to another life.

I used to teach music in Auroville schools, but I didn't really enjoy teaching children and prefer red adults. If my students didn't practice and put their hearts into it I quickly gave them up as I demanded high standards of commitment.

But I needed the teaching, as I discovered that if I did not have enough contact with people I would get out of touch and lose contact with society. Auroville is not a place for cave dwellers.

I feel from looking at the character of my kids they will eventually go out of Auroville and may not come back. Not because they are not very happy here, but because they have an ambitious streak and Auroville cannot fulfil this need. It is as if there is no "audience" here.

Tina and I always decided we would not take a maintainance here. By nature we are both freelancers and have always had a high degree of freedom in our lives. That is why I have never been in an orchestra, as I always needed the independence of doing my own thing. I give my teaching free as a gift to Auroville but demand high standards from my students.

Since 1999 we have had a recording studio and by doing graphic design work and other things we have always managed to bring enough money into Auroville to support our family of six people. We do what many people do here, and that is bring money into Auroville to support and nourish it like a child. It in return nourishes me. It gives me a vaster and wider life and a purity which is often extraordinary. It is like being a father; it is good yoga to be a father as the child turns the ego away from itself, as if the smile of a baby or the admiration of your child loosens your ego and nourishes you. Nowadays I get the urge to create something beautiful; the need for admiration and response is much less. I am fascinated by the image of beauty and truthfulness that art can create.

I have experienced many intense disappointments over my 19 years here, and looking back I can see that many of them were due to my misconceptions. I somehow had this ridiculous idea that Aurovilians were superior people, and it took me a few knocks to realize they were just the same as anywhere else. Auroville was not particularly a better place, but it definitely was a special place due to the influence and inspiration of the Mother and Sri Aurobindo. I sometimes feel many people are disappointed here, as things are not as predicted in the early seventies. Difficulties with organizations like the Town Planning for example, I feel may stem from some people's disappointment that the town is growing very slowly.

If I had the time and the money I would now like to see more of the world, hopefully in connection with my music. Tina and I went recently to Myanmar and it was a wonderful trip. We felt refreshed with the completely different environment and meeting different people. When you live in Auroville for many years you can long for the stimulation of different faces and situations.

Sri Aurobindo said some beautiful things about he role of the artist in society and I find them very inspiring. "The function of the artist is to be a seer, a visionary, who enables people to widen their spirit. To take them to places they otherwise would not reach." This is what I aim for in my music.

Tina and Holger

The Mother on music

To keep your music or writing is always good, for your nature finds its inborn occupation and that helps to maintain the vital energy and keep the balance. Why not do your sadhana through your music? Meditation is not the only way of doing sadhana. Through your music, bhakti and aspiration can grow.

ASHOK ... WHO CAME FROM NORTH INDIA IN 1990

My father was one of the lucky ones who were picked out by the British, and in 1920 went to Leeds University in Yorkshire, England. On his return he was posted in Rajasthan and joined the Indian educational service, which was of course controlled by the British. I was born in Bengal, but grew up in Rajasthan, and in 1947 I decided to join the army.

There were border problems in India at the time and many internal problems, and I thought this would be the best way to serve the country I loved. Surprisingly, many years later, it was this sense of love of service that brought me to Auroville. After all, what is a sadhak but one who aspires for a higher cause, with discipline and no self interest. I think 75% of army life can be sadhak training. My last appointment was in charge of the Indian Peace Keeping Force in Sri Lanka at a very turbulent time. I would fly from Colombo to Madras to Poona to Delhi, and when it was dark I slept, and when it was light I woke up, and often said, "Where am I?" I would sometimes lose all sense of time and place with the hectic life, and so I looked forward very much to the occasional week end with General Tewari and his family, who were living in Auroville. My personal helicopter would bring me to Pondicherry, and then I would go and sit under the banyan tree and watch Matrimandir growing.

Each time I sat there the inner truth touched me, and my soul aspired. I realized that Mother and Sri Aurobindo had given the responsibility of evolution to each person. They were very clear that it is your responsibility to seek for yourself. I had this strong feeling that if we are still evolving, we move from a vital life to a mental life, a life of knowledge and light that will lead us to the Supreme and the Divine. Here I was, living a deeply professional life in charge of thousands of men, amongst the most intense surroundings, and yet these thoughts had come to me sitting under the banyan tree ... surely grace had come from somewhere ... and I must obey its call. I still remember a senior Aurovilian

Ashok

walking back with me from the banyan tree and jokingly or sarcastically saying, "We need soldiers here, not generals." I replied to him, "When I started my life I was a soldier, and now I am going to be Mother's soldier." I live my life as if I am a young recruit, trying to learn another aspect of life. I know that is what keeps me going. In 1990 I came to live here.

What touched me the most was the words of the beautiful Auroville Charter: "Auroville belongs to no-one ... unending education ... a youth that never ages ..." Yes, they are catch words, but they give a direct connection to the work. Speaking frankly, God has been very kind to me. I am now 76 years of age, and not looking for creature comforts. What better place is there on this earth than Auroville to follow one's spiritual life? It is such a lovely place. Where on earth can I meet such a cross section of people from all over the world?

Talking with Ashok after 19 years

Initially I was in teaching and administration, but now I am involved with SAIIER, in educational and cultural work. I also look after a guest house and cultural activities in Bharat Nivas. For years the politics drew me, but nowadays I find they drain me. I resigned from the Land Consolidation Group last year when I realize it was sapping too much of my energy. I feel as if in this fourth stage of my life I am moving towards new ideas and a new way of life, and I need the mental and emotional space.

Auroville is very much still evolving, and this is why there are often such conflicts of interest which seem justifiable and inevitable when we understand the situation within this framework. Young people demand a better quality of life than we had; middle aged people with families need security; and the older people want an opportunity to develop their spirituality. These three aspects cannot be brought under one common platform, as the requirements are conflicting. If we have faith that these three requirements will be met, not in our text book way, but by higher forces, all will be well. I feel Auroville is not growing because we are now at a temporary evolutionary stage. Younger people feel insecure, and this makes them want to control. They need to feel, "This is my house." And if people leave because they do not have a good standard of living, they cannot line their own nest, then maybe they were not here for the right reason. When a house is built there is much friction and sandblasting of the bricks, many are wasted and rejected in the process; a building has to go through a lot before it is stable and upright. Auroville is like that too.

Yes, I feel Auroville is the loveliest place on earth.

VLADIMIR ... WHO CAME FROM THE UKRAINE IN 1992

I was born in the Ukraine – which used to be part of the Soviet Union – and my father was part of the "intelligentsia" and a propagandist for atheism. He was a scholar and wrote several books on history and philology and translated ancient texts. I have obviously followed in his footsteps to some extent, and he was very proud of me.

My mother used to go to church secretly, as many Russians did in those days, and sometimes took me with her. I found it a very strange mixture of a performance, with strange sounds and smells, and the cross reminded me of a graveyard. The priests served the purposes of the communist party, and I saw them as corrupt and hypocritical.

I studied English in the university, and then in 1980, when I was eighteen years old, was sent as a soldier to Afghanistan. The experience of war was horrific, though I found the country and the people beautiful. When I came back home my experiences in Afghanistan made me realize that there must be something else in life with meaning, and my conscious life began seeking knowledge.

At that time in the Soviet Union philosophical books were banned and one could go to prison if found reading Sri Aurobindo, and this as late as 1990. As I was a university student I was somehow able to find some old texts on the Kabbalah and occultism, but only through trusted friends. A group of us started "Samizdat", which means "self production" as an underground, illegal press. There were so many of us and so few books that often we only had one night to read them. When I read Sri Aurobindo's "Essays On The Gita" I clutched it to my heart as it was so precious to me. I clearly understood the power of books. The discovery of Dr. Radhakrishna's wonderful volumes of Indian philosophy and history opened my conciousness to India. I realized that when you are looking, you will find. In fact, it is difficult to avoid.

When I first came to India I was amazed to see these philosophical books being sold everywhere and just taken for granted. I came as an exchange student on a cultural programme and was in the very last batch before the collapse of the Soviet Union. I was lucky, and stayed in Poona University studying Sanskrit for one year, which I enjoyed immensely.

When I was finally able to come to Pondicherry I remember flying over Delhi on the journey here, looking out of the window and seeing the red soil, and saying to myself, "Where do I know it from?" It seemed wonderfully familiar to me. I arrived at Pondicherry in the middle of the night; everything was very calm and felt like absolute magic.

It was as if India was giving me a wonderful welcome.

I stayed at the Ashram for a while and saw how dedicated to the yoga they were, but after a short time I felt that there was really nothing going on for me there, as if everyone was doing his own thing and there was nothing I could fully engage myself in.

In 1992 I came to Auroville, and immediately felt that I had finally arrived where I wanted to be. I felt that I was here, and there was no need to go anywhere else.

Vladimir

Talking to Vladimir after 15 years

I have now been here for 15 years, and the challenges I have faced have been the best and the worst of my life. At first the main problem was that the Entry Group did not accept that teaching Sanskrit, which is what I did and what I do in life, was considered as a "proper job." However, I decided to go ahead and teach it unofficially, as the Mother and I consider it to be of great importance to the development of Auroville.

I originally studied Sanskrit in depth to be able to go deep into Savitri in the light of Sri Aurobindo. I must have taught a hundred students over the years and it has been a wonderful experience. I have also taught the Vedas, Upanishads and the Mahabharata to classes at Savitri Bhavan, where I spend a lot of my waking time putting these ancient classics on the computer.

Six years ago there seemed to be a move in Auroville to learn Sanskrit, but it has now died down, which is very disappointing. It is difficult to say why this is, except that it is a difficult task and requires great commitment. Nevertheless, I am still going on as this is my reason for being here.

The Mother on Sanskrit

If only one language is taught, it should be international. But for the general development of students, several languages are needed.

Sanskrit should be the real national language. It is only Sanskrit which will be ultimately acceptable to the people of India. Sanskrit is the only language which creates an equal handicap for all the parts of the country, so that nobody has a natural advantage over others in learning it. When I speak of Sanskrit, it should be simple Sanskrit, but not "simplified."

When India goes back to her soul, Sanskrit will naturally become India's national language. Everybody should learn Sanskrit. Especially all those who work here should learn it ... each and everyone, whatever his place of birth. Not Sanskrit on a scholarly level, but a Sanskrit which opens the door to all languages of India. I think that is indispensable. The ideal would be to have in a few years a modernized Sanskrit, that is to say, a spoken Sanskrit, like the Sanskrit you find behind all languages of India. Because now of course English is the language of the country as a whole, but that's abnormal. It is very good to facilitate relations with the rest of the world, but just as every country has its own language, India should ... But then here, the minute one wants to have a language for the whole country, everybody starts quarrelling. Everybody wants his own language to be the only one, which is stupid. But Sanskrit, no one would object to it, and it is a language more ancient than the others, in which you find the sounds, the "root-sounds" of many words.

That is something I studied with Sri Aurobindo which of course is very interesting. There are even those roots that are found in all languages of the world, root-sounds that are in all languages. Well, that is what should be learned, what should be the country's language. Every child born in India must know that, just as every child born in France must know French ... Even now, people get bogged down in quarrels, which is a very bad atmosphere to build anything. But I hope a day will come when that is possible.

CHRISTINE ... WHO CAME FROM GERMANY IN 1995

As a young child I used to love being alone, to be in silence. I remember sitting for hours on my little chair with my cat on my knee, just dreaming. I used to wear long dresses when no one else was wearing them. I loved sweet coconut candies. It was as if I had a connection with something from another life, another place.

Once I had a chance of a very good job in Africa, but I knew it was not the way for me; somehow it didn't resonate with my deepest feelings. When I eventually retired from my job as a house mother and an art and craft teacher in a boarding school I started to look for somewhere I could live comfortably on my small pension. I looked around France, but I never felt at home there.

One day I picked up a copy of "The Autobiography of a Yogi" and felt a whole new world open up to me. Suddenly everything changed. I felt I could really start living now. I wanted to go to his Ashram, but ladies were not allowed to go there on their own at that time, and I was bitterly disappointed. I came to visit Auroville, and was very impressed with what I saw and I wanted to stay here. When I told the Entry Group about my deep connection with Yogananda, they suggested that I go and live in his Ashram as that would be a more suitable place for me than Auroville.

But I decided to stay in Auroville as a long term guest and taught pottery to the Tamil village children. This had been my original idea, to help Indian children whom I loved. I felt I had been given so much in my life from my contact to India that I wanted to do something for the children as a thanks, out of a gratitude. I established a pottery in New Creation School, and now two of my students are grown men and run their own pottery business. Another one is a teacher, and I feel very proud that I have been able to help them.

At that time New Creation Field was literally just a field. I had a house built there using unfired brick, the very first house to be built in Auroville using this method. Many years later it is still in an excellent condition and is occupied by Swiss Martin and eight Tamil children and that makes me very happy.

Christine left Auroville for good in 2003 when she was 73. She had always spent the summers back in Germany, as she found the long hot summers unbearable, and each year on her return found the practicalities of living here more and more difficult. She felt nervous on her bicycle, on the sandy roads and facing the dangerous traffic of the main road. .

Although the Tamil family she had built a house for and lived above were very kind to her, she found the struggle of daily life in such a such a different culture more and more strenuous. She spoke German, and English was always an effort for her. Her Tamil was non existant and so relationships were not always spontaneous or easy for with these limitations.

She is now eighty three and is always very happy to come back to Auroville in the winter months whenever she is able.

Christine, like many older foreigners,, gave a lot to Auroville. She created a pottery school that still flourishes and is always full of happy children making clay crocodiles or Ganeshas. She inspired and supported at least two young Tamil men to develop ceramics, and now they both run their own successful businesses. Selveraj, a bright young Tamil man, caught her imagination 10 years ago, and she taught him English then sponsored him for several years. Now he is an excellent teacher in New Creation school and is training other teachers.

Christine, in her quiet and discreet way, is an example of the many people who have passed through Auroville over the years and enriched it by their creativity and generosity.

KALSANG ... WHO WAS BORN IN TIBET
AND CAME FROM DHARAMSALA IN 1995

In 1983 when the Chinese invaded Tibet my father brought myself, my twin sister and my elder brother over the Himalayas from Tibet to safety in India. It must have been an incredibly hard journey for him. After seeing us settled in the Tibetan Children's Village School in Dharamsala, he walked back to Tibet. I didn't see him again for many years.

This school, founded by our spiritual leader His Holiness the Dalai Lama, was now our home. Everything we are, or know, is due to the grace of this place, and we grew up with a good, strong heart. But it was always sad to be without a parent, especially at the holiday times, when parents would come and take their children away and we would be left behind. It was never explained to us why we were living there in that place; nobody ever thought to tell us. It was only when I was about thirteen and someone talked about Tibet's political problems and I saw some photographs, that I began to understand why we were living in India, away from Tibet and our family.

One day I was called to the school office to meet my sponsors, a French couple who had come to meet me. I can still remember my feelings of joy and gratitude to them. I felt so proud that someone cared for me, that someone had come all this way to visit me and that I was important to someone. I just hope that one day I will be able to help Tibetan children like they helped me.

When I was seventeen a French Aurovilian lady called Ann Riquier came to our school offering vocational training for two students in Auroville in South India. One position was for a cook and the other for a gardener. As I had my own little vegetable garden and loved gardening I applied for the gardening course. Many other students also applied, but one by one they dropped out when they realized the difficulties they might have. I had only read about South India from my geography books, so knew it was a very hot land where people

Kalsang

wear no shoes, sit on the ground, eat very hot curry, and eat off banana leaves. It was a four-day train journey down to Tamil Nadu, and I thought my heart would break when I said goodbye to my brother and sister. Here I was, starting a new life again, and this time completely alone. I deeply felt that this life's karma was too bitter for me.

Ann put me in Kottakarai guest house, and I stayed there for a few days just hanging about, as no one came to see me. I slowly began to realize this place was very different from what I had expected. I thought there would be forms to fill in and classes to attend, but nothing happened. I was terribly homesick, and felt like going home back to Dharamsala. I spoke very little English, couldn't ride a bicycle, and had no confidence at all. After a few days of this I decided I had to do something for myself, so I somehow found my way to Matrimandir nursery and asked for work. I worked hard, but did not receive any training, and the heat affected me and I got prickly heat and boils and headaches with the hot sun.

This was my introduction to Auroville; difficult due to my misinterpretation of the course and hard because of my loneliness.

Talking to Kalsang after 13 years

I have now been here thirteen years, and am happily married with a three year old daughter. We lived in Aspiration at first, which is very much a family community, and were very happy in that atmosphere. Then Claude, a French man who had a deep love of Tibet, began to build the Tibetan Pavilion, and asked us if we would live there as its caretakers. And so we moved there in 2000, the first settlers in the International Zone. Again my life changed completely, as I felt it was a great responsibility, and also an honour.

Auroville had been training Tibetans in building ferro-cement roofs and mud block technology, so they could work on their community monastery in Karnataka. A few years ago the Dalai Lama visited their centre to celebrate the Kalachakra inauguration. I was fortunate to be asked to attend, and was very happy also as my sister would be there whom I had not seen for several years. Everyone was waiting in a line for the Dalai Lama's blessing, and when it was my turn he looked right at me, probably because I was the only Tibetan in the line. He asked me where I came from, and when I told him about Auroville he said, "Very good, Auroville is a beautiful place, I have visited it myself twice. You are doing good work; we need more Tibetans there."

Since that moment I have been able to dedicate myself to the Tibetan Pavilion and to Auroville.

SHANKAR ... WHO CAME FROM KUILAPALAYAM VILLAGE NEAR AUROVILLE IN 1995

I was born in 1966 in the village of Kuilapalayam, which at that time was a very small, dry, farming village. My parents were farmers and had five children and we spent all our childhood looking after our land and cows.

I remember at that time the land was so flat and barren we could see our animals many kilometers away, right up to Samriddhi. That was the first bit of shade, and if they strayed further we would climb up a tamarind tree to see them. My Mother sent us to the local primary school because we were always getting into trouble, and it was free; later I went to college in Pondicherry and got a M.Phil. in economics, and then a M.Phil. in Tamil.

Life at that time was very hard for the villagers. I remember there was only one well and my mother hardly slept at night because if she didn't get to the well very early, there would be no water left. The long walk down to Repos was the only other source of water for the village. The animals drank out of the pond and the women washed the clothes in the pond and I remember our clothes were always red from the dirt. When Auroville created a better water supply my mother said that they were maharajas for bringing us clean water. Our food was very limited and monotonous; we lived mainly on varagu rice and ragi and kombu porridge and curd. In season we had fruits from the local trees such as noongu, palmyra fruit, cashew apples, jackfruit and mango.

New moon day was a feast day and so once a month we had iddlies. When I look at photos of how we were then I see skinny kids with sores at the corners of their mouths and dry hair, which signifies malnutrition. We wore skimpy loin cloths, and the last time I looked at these pictures we all looked like something in the National Geographic magazine.

Auroville started when I was two years old, so I grew up wondering who these strange white people were. I couldn't understand how the white kids could speak English so easily when they were so young, and I desperately wanted their nice food. We all thought they were crazy, as they were imitating Tamil people by dressing like us when they had all those beautiful trousers. They planted completely useless trees that bore no fruit, which seemed utterly mad to us. They seemed incredibly rich and silly and didn't know what to do with themselves and couldn't talk in our language. I remember a gang of us throwing stones at Cristo's Bullet motorbike, and he jumped off and chased us and we ran for our lives. If our parents had seen us they would have beaten us for being so stupid. I remember we would catch lizards from the pond and baby parrots and sell them to the white people for fifty paise each. They would take them away and release them. We thought they must be mad!

When I started working for Auroville my father thought I must be a lazy man, as if you didn't work with a mumpti you weren't working, and he was very disappointed in me.

As a teenager I used to teach Tamil language in Meenakshi's school, Ilaignarkal, and then go to the college in Pondicherry. I later taught Tamil in the Ashram

Shankar

school and was paid seventy rupees a month. Before and after college I had to milk my father's seven cows and collect grass for them. It was as if I had two completely separate lives going on at the same time.

It took me seven years to finish my college degree under these conditions. I never thought of joining Auroville as I didn't have clue what it was all about. I saw the pictures of Mother and Sri Aurobindo everywhere, and all the books, but none of it made any sense to me. I remember thinking, human unity.... what's that? Gradually an understanding came to me as I read Ramakrishna and Vivekananda, and travelled around south India visiting temples. As I began to explore my little part of the world I began to see how people were very different from each other. Even twenty kilometers away from Kuilapalayam the dialect was different and I remember thinking how strange that was. Kerala and Andra Pradesh were very different again, with varying traditions and customs, and I began to perceive a need for human unity to bridge these superficial differences. This eventually led me to see Auroville in a new light, and I started to take a deeper interest in the place that had been on my doorstep all my life.

In 1995 I joined Auroville. It was a great leap from my old thoughts and my life across the road in the village.

Talking with Shankar after 13 years

Looking back on my 13 years in Auroville, it has been a mixture of many things. Before I came here I was obviously a Hindu, as everyone was, though after some sitting meditation I could feel my mind opening up to something else. When I became an Aurovilian the world of Mother and Sri Aurobindo was revealed to me and I found it easy to accept them. In fact the words "Mother and Sri Aurobindo" have become my mantra, and the more I learn about the mantra the more happy I will be.

My parents live with my family of two sons. They don't really like living or being involved in Auroville as they think other villagers will feel they have no money and have to go to the "vellakaras" to beg for a more comfortable life. If we lived in the village like everyone else they would be more proud. If I try to explain that it is the place of Mother and Sri Aurobindo and we are trying to live a different way of life, they think I am crazy.

I used to teach Tamil to foreigners, which I love doing, but for three years now I have been Principal of New Creation School. I hate to spend four or five hours a day doing administration and trying to sort everyone out; what I want to do is be with the children whom I love. I have been to the USA three times to teach a term of Tamil culture in a university, which is a great way to get some money and see the world. This last time I saw snow, which was amazing. My real love however is teaching the Tamil language and culture, and I hope I can do more of this in the future as I feel there is a real need for it.

I feel I have missed absolutely nothing by living in Auroville. My life style and understanding of things is worth a billion euros more than what I could have earned outside Auroville. I want to pass the rest of my days being an Aurovilian, and I would like to sleep in Adventure cremation ground at the end of my days.

RICARDO ... WHO CAME FROM ARGENTINA IN 1997

I have no childhood memories of religion ever being discussed in our house, although my mother was a practising Roman Catholic and my father was a Jewish agnostic. I awoke to spiritually in my teens and became fascinated by philosophy, but never connected it with a search for God. I read Karl Marx, Hegel, and then graduated on to Herman Hesse and eventually to Krishnamurti, who made a lot of sense to me.

At university I studied architecture, but had to stop when my father suddenly died and we were in financial difficulties. I became an airline pilot, which was my boyhood dream, and I loved it. I remember those long flights sitting in the cockpit looking at the stars; they were so much bigger and brighter up there. And the curve of the roundness of the earth and the sheer immensity of the creation constantly amazed me. The technical challenge of taking off and landing a huge plane used to thrill me. It was a wonderful career.

But in 1975 life in Argentina became unbearable, when the dictator Videla took over. I fled to Europe to escape the horrors, but was unable to work as a pilot there because of my nationality. After a few years I returned to Argentina and lived up in the Cordova mountains. I started a new life with a small farm and worked in leather and learned carpentry, which I have been doing ever since.

One day, out of the blue, I had an experience which changed my life. My partner had gone away to Buenos Aires for a few weeks and I was staying alone on my farm. I decided to take my backpack and spend the day walking by the river. Suddenly, as I was walking up a mountain path, a force stopped me in my tracks and I felt as if a voice was saying: "Why didn't you see me before?" I was absolutely stunned, and started to cry with emotion. Then I felt as if I could see God manifest in the trees and the animals, and that I absolutely knew the reason for everything.

Ricardo

Afterwards I became like a man in a fever and searched all the book shops trying to find out if others had had this experience. I discovered Carlos Castaneda, especially the "Second Ring of Power," and then "The Autobiography of a Yogi". In retrospect I think the pilot in me had been crying out because he could not fly the skies, although I felt happy in my new farming life.

My partner Sylvia was a Catholic and she was very supportive of me; we used to practice hatha yoga together. She belonged to a yoga group that went to India every year, and I desperately wanted to go with her, but could not leave the farm. Then Sai Baba came into my life – in the spirit. I had met several of his devotees and was very impressed with their dedication. One told me, "If you think of him with all your heart, he will let you know he is there. But be careful, he has a strong presence and he will play games with you."

I was eventually able to come to India, stayed in his ashram for four glorious months, and had first-hand experience of his miracles. I do believe he is an avatar, and when I was in his presence I felt as if I had gone to Paradise. I also fell in love with India. I felt everything was alive here, as if the people were touched by a spirituality. I asked Sai Baba if I should come and live here. He closed his eyes for a few minutes and then said, "You can do with your life whatever you want."

I had to return to Argentina, however, and began to work for myself as a carpenter. One day, on my way to work in the morning, I stopped at a little shop to buy some maté tea and biscuits. I got chatting to the man who served me, as you do, and I must have mentioned India, as he suddenly said, "Hey, I've got a girl staying here whose sister, Prema, is living somewhere in India called Auroville, and she wants to send something to her. Maybe you can help her." I met the girl, promised to take the parcel to India for her, and that was the first time I heard of Auroville.

After a couple of years I was able to return to India, and visited Ramana Maharshi's ashram in Tiruvannamalai. Staying next door to me was Karuna, who lived in Samriddhi community, and she told me a lot about Auroville, how it was developing and how she loved it, and I felt this strong pull towards it. Again I had to return to Argentina, but after one year I was able to finally come to Auroville, and arrived on Mother's birthday with three hundred dollars in my pocket.

Here I felt my life had finally started. It had been a long and circuitous route.

Talking to Ricardo after 11 years

I have now been here 11 years and have often found it full of difficulties, or challenges as I prefer to call them. I feel I have been able to face them with courage and hope due to the Divine grace, and honestly feel I am a blessed man. That is why I called my carpenter's workshop "New Dawn", because that is what my life has been here. I first worked in Surrender, then started a workshop outside Auroville, then got a loan and created "New Dawn" at Kottakarai.

I think my main achievement here is my relationship with my Tamil workers. Many of them have been here with me for years as "thambis", young boys, and I have trained them; now they are professional carpenters. They have been my teachers in many ways, on a human and a carpentry level. They are capable of doing very fine work and are loyal and honest. I have created a co-op which belongs to us all and it works very well. We must have worked on at least 300 Aurovilian houses and have never had any complaints. I sometimes go out and work in Bangalore and Chennai, but I don't like to leave my place; except the money is useful as a boost to the business.

I often feel very disturbed by people's attitude to the Tamils. We have had millennia of superiority that has become an ancestral problem as it has been going on so long. We have become used to being the boss and it is difficult to change. When I hear the minimum wage in Auroville is 83 rupees for a day's work, and I know people who are paying their ammas 50 rupees a day, I get angry. Westerners say things like, "They are always asking for money, I don't like it." If they just thought for a minute how difficult it can be for many Tamils on such a low wage, they would realise how they are forced to ask for help. I have often had to ask Auroville for help; everyone needs to be able to ask at some time. I have learned that the best way to deal with these requests is to have a limit, write everything down, and then deduct it from their "sambalam" every week.

My life changed very much last year when my 84-year-old mother from Argentina came to live with me. My house is in the green belt at the end of a very narrow lane, inaccessible to taxis, so it was difficult for her to go anywhere. Also she did not speak a single word of English, and there are very few Spanish speaking people here. My amma was sympathetic to her, but of course she did not speak English, and I was out working most of the time, so she became lonely. She went back to Argentina to live with my brother, but now she says she finds it even more lonely there, as he lives in a city and is out working all day for long hours. I get disturbed when I think about her, and have asked her if she would like to come out here again. The latest plan is that my brother will take leave from his job and come out here with our mother and stay for a year. That will change my life a lot. The responsibility for elderly parents in far away countries is a difficult situation that many older Aurovilians have to face, and usually involves a lot of coming and going. I know several people who have brought their parents to live out here, with varying degrees of success. I trust that Mother will give me the patience and kindness of heart to do my duty well.

MARTIN ... WHO CAME FROM SWITZERLAND IN 1997

In the early 1970s I remember seeing pictures in a German magazine of people digging an enormous hole in South India. I was amazed and touched by their effort, then I forgot about it.

As a child I was always fascinated by pictures of India, but was always a little afraid of the vastness of the country and the crowds and the poverty. As a young adult I travelled to many countries but always avoided India, as if it were too much for me, too special for me, as if I was not yet ready for it.

In 1985 I came to Pondicherry and stayed at the Ashram. I was very impressed with the older women; there was something special about them, a dignity and a sense of poise and purpose that I had not come across before. I used to read the Indian newspapers in the Ashram Library and these women were always so attentive and caring to me. I remember buying a beautiful yellow bedspread in the Auroville Boutique, and whenever I looked at it over the years, the depth and quality of it always gave me a very good feeling.

Before I came to Auroville I had read some of Sri Aurobindo's books in German but found them difficult to understand. At that time I hadn't even heard of Mother and I remember asking someone, "Who is that old lady" when I saw a picture of her. Years later I read the books again in English, and occasionally had that wonderful feeling when hidden things are suddenly revealed and everything is brilliantly clear.

My wife and I read about Auroville again in a German magazine when we were travelling in Rajasthan. It was one of those glossy magazines with lots of photos that you see lying around in hotels. There were pictures of bullock carts and strange, exotic houses and it looked fascinating. I think the article was called, "The Vision is Blooming.", and it made us want to know more and maybe even go and visit "The City of the Future."

Unfortunately we had no money at the time as we were living hand to mouth, so we couldn't even think of going all that way to South India. But we really had set our hearts on going, so in our desperation one day we asked Mother;"If you want us to go to Auroville, please help us." Miraculously, within weeks I got a pension from an old job and my wife got some money from her grandmother. We were rich! We set off for Auroville.

When we finally did get to Auroville we immediately loved it. We especially loved the combination of Auroville and India. I had always been fascinated by the details of India; a mother in a red sari feeding her child by hand... a white bullock sitting by the road...there seemed to be a hidden world in these Indian details of life. Life here seems very human, both in an extremely positive and negative way. It is sometimes tough, but it always looks you in the eye; it is not wishy-washy, you can't arrange or control it and on that level it is very honest. Maybe all this is a reaction to my being Swiss. I don't know.

All I do know is that I cannot imagine Auroville being anywhere else in the world but India.

Talking to Martin after 11 years

When I came here 11 years ago I had a very smooth landing. I felt at home and nothing was difficult. I started work in Forecomers nursery though I knew absolutely nothing of Indian flora and fauna, but felt good when after a few months I knew the names and habit of all this tropical greenery.

I was fascinated by the local Tamil culture and would have far preferred to live in the village of Kuilapalayam instead of Auroville, but that was not allowed. I always have felt attached to these people and comfortable with them, as if I am "at home". Maybe this is because in Switzerland I worked for a while with the Red Cross and got to know Sri Lankan refugee Tamils and liked them a lot.

Then for 6 years I worked in New Creation doing the dinners for the staff and children. I enjoyed the work very much, though never could learn Tamil. I found the villagers spoke a strange and incomprehensible dialect that was very difficult to follow, and they could never explain Tamil words to me. I went to Tamil classes but the teacher was a Tamil who did not understand westerners, and on the first lesson gave us 30 Tamil words to learn. Of course nobody did, and the teacher never came again. I tried another class but the teacher talked about nouns and adverbs and at that time my English was poor and I didn't know what he was talking about, so that didn't last long either.

I am now working at the Matrimandir nursery. On my third day there I was suddenly told, in true Auroville fashion:"You're in charge now; of the plumeria collection." After the initial panic, as I knew absolutely nothing of plumerias, I became fascinated by them and we now have a world famous collection of plumerias. We have 220 different varieties and have them catalogued in a digital library. Each tree is photographed from different angles and always has a person standing beside it to indicate the size of the tree. Narad is the soul behind this and we have become world experts. The Japanese love them and often come and give 2,000 rupees for a cutting. Last month one man took 14 cuttings so we felt very proud.

When I was working at New Creation kitchen I was often approached by village people and asked if I would take in a child who was homeless. When I saw these kids living in the most appalling circumstances I felt I should help, and took four little girls in. Part of my reason was to give my two boys the opportunity to live with Tamil people and learn some of their different qualities. It worked out really well most of the time, as in all families, and I am so glad I did it. Now my family has increased to eight, as two years ago I married Shivakala from the village who has a little boy.

We got married in true Tamil style in the temple and her family at first was very confused. They knew she wasn't marrying me for my money as I made it clear to them I only receive 3,000 rupees a month maintenance and therefore could not support her cousins and uncles and aunties and finance weddings. I am sure they could not understand why she was marrying me. But they are happy now, especially as they don't have to support her son with school fees. The children are sponsored by British and Swiss people and somehow that always seems to work out, though as they are getting older things often get tight. Some of the cultural differences have had to be sorted out when we started living together. For example, she is easily drawn into the village family life with all its complications, so I have had to explain our different way of living and that her first priority is her New Creation Field family. She is learning English and we communicate in weird and wonderful ways. It is very, very nice being married to Shivakala.

Somehow my dream has come true.

Martin

The Mother on India

From time immemorial (some scholars say 8,000 years before the Christian era) India has been the land of spiritual knowledge and practice, of the discovery of the Supreme Reality and union with it.

India is not the earth, rivers and mountains of this land, rather it is a collective name for the inhabitants of this country; India is a living being, as much living as, say, Shiva. India is a goddess as Shiva is a god. If she likes, she can manifest in human form.

Spiritual aspiration develops very strongly and spontaneously as soon as one comes to India. Those are graces, Graces, because it is the destiny of the country, it has been so throughout her history, and because she has always been turned much more upward and inward than outward, She is now losing all that and wallowing in the mud, but anyway ... it was like that and still is like that.

The future of India is very clear. India is the guru of the world. The future structure of the world depends on India. India is the living soul. She incarnates the spiritual knowledge in the world. The government of India ought to recognize this significance of India in this sphere and plan their action accordingly ...

Divine power alone can help India. If you can build faith and cohesion in the country it is much more powerful than any man-made power. According to a very old tradition, if twelve honest persons unite to incarnate the divine Will, they can compel the Divine to manifest ... There must be a group forming a strong body of cohesive will with the spiritual Knowledge to save India and the world. It is India that can bring Truth in the world. By manifestation of the divine Will and Power alone India can preach her message to the world and not by imitating the materialism of the West. By following the divine Will India shall shine at the top of the spiritual mountain and show the way of Truth and organize world unity.

DEEP ... WHO CAME FROM CALCUTTA IN 1998

When I was in Calcutta ten years ago I discovered Mother's Agenda on the internet, and somehow got the idea that she was going to start a community somewhere outside Pondicherry. I got the impression it never happened, as I had never heard of Auroville, although Bangalore is quite near Pondicherry. It was finally the Tourist Agency who told me, yes, it did exist, and its name was Auroville. I looked it up on the internet and immediately wanted to visit this strange place called Auroville. At that time I was doing my Ph.D. in maths at Bangalore University. I was going through a phase of losing interest in the subject and the sort of life it would eventually lead me into, with all its ambitions and materialism.

On my first vacation I came and spent a week here, and straight away responded to the beauty of Auroville. I loved the space and the trees and the openness of the people. To discuss spiritual matters seemed very natural here. In Bangalore I felt isolated, as these things were considered rather weird, not conducive to a modern, ambitious computer man's life. I then started reading Mother and Sri Aurobindo's books and realized I had found my soul-mates; I wanted to be part of the Sri Aurobindo movement and the actual process of living it. In the big city this is very difficult to do, as the spiritual path just seems to become yet another part of a busy and full life.

I realized why I had never heard of Auroville when I lived not so far away from it in Bangalore. Firstly, I couldn't find it! It is hidden away from the main road with only a small rickety signpost for directions, and it is sort of camouflaged with the local villages. There seem to be no gates or boundaries ... no actual beginnings or endings. It is very private, it never publicises itself. Even when I lived there, I used to think: "Where do all these people live? Where do they all go when they disappear down those tracks?" It was all so discreetly quiet about itself.

When I made my decision to come and live here my tutor was shocked, my mother very sad, and my father furious. They just could not understand. They saw a wonderful career being thrown away after so many years of study and hard work. I think my mother understands a little now: I do hope so.

I tell her; " Here I can breathe differently ." It was written on the wall.

SARASIJA ... WHO CAME FROM SOUTH KOREA IN 1999

My father was a government official, a simple, silent man, always hiding behind his newspaper and television. It was my mother who inspired my life. She was always cooking or creating a beautiful garden and I had the feeling as a child that I was held in her hands. It was she who inspired me to find my own unique way in the world.

Thanks to her I went to Art School and studied sculpture for four years. I then married and had a little boy. My dear mother had always taken me to the temple, and one of my dreams was to fulfil the Buddhist's vision of visiting Buddhist temples on a pilgrimage, especially in India. However, it took me fifteen years to get to India. It always seemed an impossibility for me with my studying and working and then having a family.

Shantiniketan, Tagore's University in Bengal, was always my idea of a dream place, so when I got the chance of studying sculpture there I was overjoyed. South Korea had respected Gandhi, and Tagore was always popular in South Korea. Indeed, he had said: "In the golden age of Asia, Korea was one of its lamp bearers. And that lamp is waiting to be lighted once again for the illumination of the East." The time I spent in Shantiniketan was life-changing for me. It was a very peaceful place with a few foreigners, and the students cycled around the spacious beautiful gardens. The standard of teaching by the Bengali teachers was very high. Dance and singing were given high priority to awaken the spirit, and the atmosphere was steeped in beauty and refinement. I had the blessing of living there for three years, and studied Indian philosophy and began to understand the Indian mind.

When my time there finished I had to return to Korea and life was completely different. I had slowed down in India, my heart and mind had moved in a calm, reflective way, but now I was thrust into competitive urban living. The way of life felt crazy; it was like living in a hell. I started an Art Institute and taught drawing, my husband lectured, and we worked a twenty four hour shift. I was caught up in this society, where we needed a house and a car and a job and savings, and I felt very stressed and isolated. One day I fainted in my art class and was diagnosed with severe exhaustion. This shocked me, and made me take stock of my life and ask myself what I really wanted? I realized I could not continue in this rat race, so decided to go back to Shantiniketan. My husband stayed behind with his teaching job, and we separated, but we are still very good friends.

Aurelio had visited South Korea and told me about Auroville in glowing terms, so I decided to visit. I immediately fell in love with it, and felt this was the place where I could develop my soul. But it was my nine year old son who made the final decision for us. He had gone to Transition School, and after a week told me; "The teachers are so gentle and loving. I really want to be here. Yes Mother, this is my place."

Talking with Sarasija after 10 years

Language has always been my greatest problem here. And the very great difference in culture from Korea. Although I lived for three years in Shantiniketan

Sarasija

in an Indian culture it did not prepare me for the very different world of the western culture of Auroville. The Korean culture is Far Eastern, with the emphasis on a more flexible and human attitude to life than that of the West, and we still have a more traditional attitude to family and friends. This difference means I have to be constantly aware not to offend, not to seem strange, not to smile too much, to give too many presents. I have to think two or three times before speaking. When we say "hello" it is "in a different atmosphere". I feel people are saying: "Why is she smiling so much, what has happened?" And next time I don't smile so much. It is as if "the French live behind French walls and the Germans live behind German walls" and I have to learn to understand this. I love the Tamil people, as I find them much easier to understand, and feel more familiar with their culture. When I came here nine years ago there were only three Korean people here, and I often felt very lonely. Now there are 25 of us and we help and support each other, which is important.

The first year was very difficult for my son as he was the first Korean student. Fortunately he was very polite and had good concentration, so the teachers were pleased with him. He is now going to high school in Korea as he wants to go to university there. My mother and brother have been here, and felt more reassured after seeing my nice house, and could see that I was not really as crazy as they had thought.

People often ask me why there are not any Japanese or Thai or Chinese people here. My personal opinion is that the Koreans are still a more spiritual race and have a more independent mind. And they have more money, which of course you need to live in Auroville. The Japanese have a very strong sense of identity and would find it difficult to surrender; also they have many communities in their country. Many Korean guests are now coming here, and I always advise them to have enough money and be very sure of their level of inspiration.

When I visited Ladakh I was fascinated by the Tibetan gompas and thankas in their temples. I started to do mandalas, which for me are like a balance of harmonies, an expression of the Divine within a circle. I now do this as my work and my service to Auroville by giving classes here to share my love of mandalas. Every two years I have an exhibition in Korea under the title of Sarasija Mandala Arts. I would love to have shows in India, but I don't know about the galleries here, and the difficulties of transporting large paintings are overwhelming. In Shantinketan I did a series of sculptures and called them my spaceship sculptures, as I had always wanted to fly, to go to other worlds in my spaceship. When I saw the Matrimandir I realized I had been sculpting it for the last few years without knowing anything about it. I felt it had been built for me, and I totally surrendered to Mother at that moment. I knew I could go to inner and outer space in this incredible building, which was here waiting for me. I shaved my head and changed my name to Sarasija, which means "water lily". This is my "delivery" name for the Mother, my name for my spaceship Mother.

I will be 50 next year, and have waited a long time for this period of my life. Now I feel I am ready to fly, to develop my spiritual life after years of caring for my son. I worked in the Nursery gardens for years and saw how the branches of the trees have to be pruned so the strength can concentrate in the trunk. That is how I feel now, that my life, like the tree, must be disciplined and harmonized.

SHAILAJA ... WHO CAME FROM BARODA, NORTH INDIA, IN 2001

My family was Brahmin Marathi and we lived in Baroda in a large joint family. In many ways it can be a good way to live, as everyone shares and experiences all stages of life – childhood, old age, widowhood, and so on, but for someone like me it was very restrictive. The personality was not allowed to be developed, as the family's good had to come first; for example, you could never have your food preferences as the whole family had to be fed, you could never do just what you wanted without many people being affected. There were about twenty people in our immediate family, but I remember when we had a puja for someone's passing, and there must have been over one hundred of my family there, I found it overwhelming. Traditionally, the son would follow in the father's footsteps, taking up his profession and living in the family home all his life. When he married he would bring his bride to join his family. The family only broke up when men had to leave to find work in another town.

Somehow I always felt that this sort of life was only a temporary arrangement for me, that I might one day leave. I didn't know how and never discussed it with anyone. It was just understood by everyone that one day I would have an arranged marriage and follow the tradition. In retrospect I knew absolutely nothing about myself, just what I had been told.

Life dramatically changed for me when I got married and left my old life behind. I was twenty two and studying architecture. My own teacher had never let me dream; everything had been for getting ahead in the profession and I could not bear this, so I became a teacher to be able to inspire others. Lalit was also an architect, from a different caste, but that did not concern us and we got married. He came to Auroville in 1999 to work on a project, and was full of wonder and surprise at its achievements. I came to join him and also loved the place, but we had no idea of staying here. We wanted to experience new places

Shailaja

and travel together. At first it just seemed like another new place, but it worked its magic on me and we stayed.

Things began to be difficult when I realized everything was different here. Up till then I had defined myself by my work, saying "I am an architect", but suddenly I knew I had to find out for myself who I really was; I had to know myself. I felt the legacy of my upbringing rapidly crumbling away; it was painful for me. I began to question everything and discuss all these new attitudes to life with trusted friends. They said things like, "I don't cook if I don't want to," and I was amazed. Lalit and I decided to share the cooking and the other domestic chores, which was unheard of in an Indian Brahmin family. The balance shifted to and fro between us, and he accepted it. It was as if I was the actor and he was the backdrop and he just gracefully let it happen.

In retrospect it took a long time for Auroville to crystallize for me, at least three years. It is as if it affects us in very different ways, depending on what the soul is asking for. That is why I love Auroville. It was only when I became pregnant that I honestly said, "Yes, I want to be an Aurovilian. I want to connect with Mother." When you are ready ... things happen. I attended talks in Last School on "The Life Divine" and began to read Sri Aurobindo and Mother avidly. I used to read them to my unborn child as we settled down like nesting birds.

Lalit and I decided to have a home birth with Lalit helping me, and my parents were horrified. It is traditional for us that the daughter returns to the parent's house two months before the birth, then stays to be cared for over another one and half months after the birth. It was very difficult for my mother, as the first child is a big event and pujas have to be done, so I promised her I would come and stay with her a few months later. When we did go to her house in Chandrigar the baby cried non-stop, but the minute we returned to Auroville she became quiet and peaceful. We called her Sagarhika, which means "of the ocean". I have always felt she has been giving me signals that this place is truly our home.

Here "All life is yoga" and you cannot escape it. It has been a slow process on the path, and I have questioned everything again and again, but now I know we are absolutely settled and meant to be here. With Mother's blessing. You know, sometimes I feel her standing over there by that building.

Talking with Shailaja after 7 years

I have now been here for seven years and sometimes find my work as an architect frustrating and difficult, mainly due to the different attitudes of people here in Auroville compared to the outside world. The work is much more demanding, as the clients have very strong ideas about what they want. The clients themselves do not pay, as the money is raised through government or fundraising, and often there can be some tricky situations. I feel as if here I have to be a sort of sociologist to understand the different cultures and expectations, a philosopher to maintain harmony in the group, and a contractor to look after the maintenance details. For example, if there is rain, I am the one who has to rush off and put a tarpaulin over the unfinished roof. Like all difficult situations, however, it is an opportunity to be creative and get a good team together and learn to dream together.

For example, I am now working on a new school. I sit together with the teachers and we discuss the plans, and I let them give their input of ideas and suggestions. We try to crystallize our plans together, and I am especially involved, as I have a seven year old daughter who attends a school. Sometimes we feel we are fumbling for ideas and I realize there are five different criteria to satisfy. Firstly, the 'client' who are the teachers who will have to work in this building, then the students who are all different ages with different needs, then the land itself. I feel as if it sits there asking for the appropriate form and shape to occupy it. Then as the building grows, it becomes an identity and shows you what it needs and wants. And then there is my own aspiration...

I have been blessed by a teacher and friend here, Helmut, an established architect who I can go to for advice when I feel confused or need encouragement. I am sure this would not happen outside Auroville, where professional people are competitive, and I think this is a wonderful thing when people share their knowledge.

My daughter Sagarhika is very happy here and now goes to Transition School, which is excellent. The educational system here supports the education that Sri Aurobindo and the Mother developed, with the child having freedom and internal discipline and joy in learning. The children seem to have a thirst for learning that is encouraged beautifully by their teachers, who know and care for them all personally.

We love living in our community of Courage and are so glad we chose to live here. I like to hear people around; I would never like to live in an isolated place. Everybody's door is open for the neighbour's children and they just go out of their front door to meet friends. I love the way the parents treat everybody's children as their own, it is a very relaxed and happy way to live. Yes, I do miss having a terrace as we are on the ground floor, and yes, it is getting far too small for us, but these are minor difficulties. And I wish the architect had included a communal dining space where we could meet our neighbours on a more regular basis or sometimes eat together .

One thing in Auroville that really affects me for three months every year is the pesticide spraying. It gives me a sore throat and a cough and my daughter often gets a high fever with it. We must do something about it once and for all. And it did take me three or four years to acclimatize to the summer humidity; at first I found the summers difficult after the dry heat of my family home, but now it is not too bad.

I insist on time for myself now. The feeling of loneliness I experienced as a child was essential to my search for finding out who I really am. Auroville gives me the support and space to do this. I get a lot of strength and nourishment from attending the Sunday morning classes run by Shraddhavan at the beautiful Savitri Bhavan. We all read from Savitri, meditate on a small passage, then contribute our understandings to the group. It now feels as if we are a Savitri family. It has such a power for me and affects the soul like nothing else. I also attend a small group run by Deepti which meets to read Sri Aurobindo together, and this gives me much support. It brings the psychic being in front.

I feel I am truly blessed to live in such a place.

VALERIA ... WHO CAME FROM ITALY IN 2002

I was born in Italy, and at the age of seventeen developed a longing for spiritual and psychological knowledge. I read Krishnamurti, Sai Baba, Vivekananda and anything I could get my hands on, which more than thirty years ago was difficult, as not many books had been translated into Italian.

When I was twenty-two a friend asked me to go to India with him, and I jumped at the idea. I immediately loved India. I didn't speak a word of English, and I remember getting locked in a bathroom and shouting for help in Italian, and how long a time it was before anyone came to rescue me. The beggars were very different from what they are now. I remember a beggar who sat at the corner of our street every day. If I gave him two rupees he would give me a beautiful smile, and if I gave him nothing he would give me the same beautiful smile. I would look into his eyes and see such peace and happiness there. I thought of my father's eyes, which rarely showed any peace of mind, although he was a successful professor and physician. I was so sad when I had to leave India.

I then had to think deeply about how I wanted to live my life. I knew for sure that I wanted to live in India, but I had no money and no profession. Somehow I just followed in my father's footsteps and studied psychology at university. When I qualified I worked in a psychiatric hospital, but I was far too young and inexperienced, and carried everyone's problems on my shoulders, and got confused and depressed.

Then a boyfriend bought a yacht and asked me to sail with him, and that was the beginning of many years sailing. On our travels I met a fascinating Japanese solo sailor called Kenji, and a few years later I bumped into him and his boat again on the Panama Canal. We became very close friends, and eventually lived and sailed together and travelled by boat to Japan. It seems strange, but I do not really enjoy sailing, even though the sailing boat was my only home for eight

Valeria

years. I get sea sick and cannot swim very well, but I do love the feeling of being on a small boat in a vast ocean surrounded only by water and sky.

We lived on a small southern island off Japan for fourteen years. At the beginning I found the Japanese people difficult to understand; sometimes they seemed to have come from another planet, as they were so different. Their language, culture, facial expressions, everything about them was utterly different. But by learning Ikebana I started to go deep into the Japanese culture and start to understand and appreciate it. Many strange behaviours suddenly were not strange anymore.

But I still desperately wanted to come and live in India, and yet here I was living in a completely opposite society. In the summer Kenji sailed our yacht, and in the winter he worked as a carpenter. I was teaching Italian and Italian cooking and trying to save money for India.

In 1991 when we were travelling around Kerala we read about a big music festival in Chidambaram, and decided we wanted to go there. Somehow we managed it, but when we arrived there were no hotels available, and then I got very sick. We decided to take a taxi to Pondicherry, where I lay in a hotel bed with a fever for days. When I recovered a little we consulted our India guide books, mine in Italian and Kenji's in Japanese, to find somewhere peaceful where I could go and recover.

Our guide books implied that Auroville was quite a bad place, with a strange Western sect and an occult guru called Mirra Alfassa. It was claiming to be a Utopia, a city of the future with drugs, alcohol and sex, and everyone had to wear white clothes and work for no money. We said we definitely were not going there. Our marital roles were now reversed, as previously I was the one who would explore new towns while Kenji liked to stay quietly in the hotel reading or watching National Geographic channel on TV. He is a very quiet person, and hates crowds and will never go in a shop, always waiting outside for me. This time things were different. One afternoon he said he was going for a walk and he was gone for hours; I was getting worried as this was very unlike him. When he eventually returned he was very excited and told me he had gone into Auroville Boutique, and I couldn't believe it. The idea of Kenji going into a boutique was unbelievable! He told me he had felt drawn in by something, and talked to the shop man and got information about this strange place Auroville. Now he wanted to go there! All this was completely out of character for him, and I was beginning to get worried at his insistence. I definitely didn't want to go out to this remote crazy place, as I was still sick, but he literally dragged me out there in a rickshaw. The boutique had given him the name of a Japanese lady called Michiko, so we called on her and she made us very welcome.

It was the 31st December, the most crowded month in Auroville, and we were told there was no chance of getting a room. A rickshaw took us through kilometres of trees to Centre Guest House where Silvano, a lovely Italian man, came out to welcome us and asked us if we were looking for a room. He happened to have a double room, as someone had just cancelled the reservation, so we stayed there for a few weeks.

It was as if Kenji had been compelled to come here and drag me along with him. As if he had been compelled to go into the smart tourist boutique and talk to the man, which was utterly against his usual nature of shyness and reticence. Definitely something, or someone, had drawn us here, almost against our will.

I had just started to learn Ikebana in Japan, and developed this strange idea that I should teach Ikebana in Auroville. This was quite ridiculous, as fifteen years ago Auroville was still very basic, and even in Pondicherry there were no suitable vases and definitely no flower shops. And I was actually not very attracted to Auroville at that time. There seemed to be little joy here, people almost didn't speak to each other at Pour Tous and the atmosphere often felt very heavy. Why were we coming to live here? We knew nothing about Mother and Sri Aurobindo and hadn't even visited the Ashram. I didn't even know Mother had lived in Japan. Yet still there was this strange, inexplicable pull. My Italian family thought I was crazy. "How can you go and teach Ikebana in a country where people are starving? Why don't you just forget all this nonsense?" But we went back to Japan and worked hard to save money in order to come and live here. I studied Ikebana for 10 years and got a diploma. We came to visit Auroville several other times, and then I found I was pregnant at 42 years of age. It was the birth of Monica that gave us the final push to come here. Kenji brought his Japanese industrial planes and saws to establish a workshop and make his beautiful furniture. There were no vases for me to start an Ikebana course, but two weeks after our arrival Michel from Flame pottery rang to say he had an order from Italy for twelve Ikebana vases, and he started to produce them for Auroville. I couldn't believe it! In a very short time I got all my needs for teaching Ikebana.

So this is how we came to Auroville. Mother dragged us here, almost against our will, mine especially.

Talking with Valeria after 6 years

We have now been here for six years and have found it a very mixed experience. I think a lot of my problems were due to a strange idea I had of Aurovilians, that they were somehow very superior people, and I was almost embarrassed to show myself in front of them. Of course this ridiculous idea came crashing down after a while, and I had to start to look inwards. I hope I am following my spiritual path ... sometimes I wonder.

My main problem here is somehow on a practical level, though I know it is in my head. I grew up in Italy, then lived in Japan for fifteen years, and now

I am living in India. Each culture gives you perspectives on many different levels, and they become part of your habitual way of thinking. Japan was a very precise and rigid country, the complete opposite of India, and I have become very Japanese. The chaos and poor workmanship of India drives me crazy. For example, yesterday my motorbike broke down, so the mechanic replaced it with another one that then broke down on the East Coast Road. My husband had to come and rescue me and I was late for a meeting. Then when I got my bike back this morning the two litres of fuel I had put in it had been stolen. Something like this seems to happen every other day, and saps my energy. My standard of order and cleanliness is very high, and the endless housework this involves irritates me. By 9 pm I am exhausted, whereas when I am in Italy or Japan I feel I am just starting the night!

We came to Auroville to live a simple life, but somehow this always eludes me, and it is as if life is more complicated here because of the inefficiency of the system. I felt so free when we left Japan and I got rid of fifteen years accumulation of possessions. Now I seem to have just as much stuff .

Thank goodness my Italian family sends me a ticket for two months each summer, as I have a crazy skin that goes into prickly heat in March. I love going to Italy, but as I have been away for twenty six years I now feel like a tourist. Last year we went to Japan, and I was surprised to feel that it still felt like "my place."

My nine year old daughter Monica loves living in Auroville. She loves the trees and the birds and the freedom. How it will be when she is a teenager, I don't know. Kenji and I did not want her to grow up in the rigid Japanese system and that was one of the reasons we came here. Again, we were full of unrealistic dreams and expectations, and were disappointed when we found that some Aurovilian children were even tougher and more quarrelsome than children elsewhere. It can be difficult for them, as there are so few of them and their lives overlap all the time. They can't go off and join, for example, a swimming club with different children, as these opportunities don't exist here. But Monica is very happy and I cannot imagine her being anywhere else.

Kenji and I work for ourselves, which has been, and still is, financially precarious. He makes beautiful tables and furniture to a very high standard, which are difficult to sell as we live in this remote spot. We displayed some tables in a Pondicherry gallery, and when the ones that did not sell were returned to us they had been damaged, as the Indians did not know how to care for and respect them. Unfortunately neither of us are good business people, and we don't have the will or expertise to find a market for these very unusual tables.

I studied Ikebana in Japan for ten years and love to run classes and teach people about this beautiful art. Again, like Kenji's furniture, it is something that only appeals to a few people, and so I am busy mainly in the guest season. I tell my students they are here to learn the basics, and should "surrender" to the rules of the art. Some Westerners find this very difficult and say things like; "I really don't like orange and blue together." They have the idea that it is like Western flower arrangement, which of course it is not. It is completely different, as its aim is to awaken the spirit and allow one to see beauty in many forms. When I first came to India I was discouraged, as there did not seem to be any real flowers here, but after a while I saw flowers everywhere, usually scattered on the ground.

I charge money for my Ikebana classes as this is how I make my living. We brought money with us from our years of working in Japan, but of course it has now all gone on paying for our house. Money is a big struggle here for us, as we don't take any maintenance and have to support ourselves. What really upsets me is when Aurovilians do not understand and accuse me, verbally or through letters, of going against the aims and ideals of Auroville by accepting money. How are we supposed to live? We contribute a lot; each month we put in 5,400 rupees into the Pour Tous account and make our 3,000 contribution to the Auroville Fund, and when I give exhibitions I pay rent for the space. I, and many other people here, am confused about Auroville's attitude to money. It is as if those with money live in a different world. When I see the people who accuse me of earning money eating at the expensive Promenade restaurant in Pondicherry I feel hurt, angry and confused. Neither Kenji nor I have a pension, and that worries us sometimes, as we are both in our late fifties.

Apart from all these "complaints," some due to my background, some because of my ridiculous high expectations, and others probably due to pure ignorance, I am very happy and grateful to be here in this place.

AVIRAM AND YORIT ... WHO CAME FROM ISRAEL IN 2002

Aviram

My life changed completely in 1997 when my company sent me to Thailand on a business trip for three days. I was working as the Chief Executive Officer of the company, and although I had travelled a lot, I had never been to the East. At the last minute Yorit, my wife, was able to join me, and together we saw a very different culture – and were captivated.

From the very first moment Bangkok was an eye-opener. The sight of Buddhist monks meditating peacefully together, people performing slow beautiful Tai Chi movements in the parks, everything was new and magnificent. We extended our trip to ten days and decided to come back as soon as we could. When we returned to Israel a friend lent me Herman Hesse's "Siddhartha", which revealed another world to me. I decided to quit my job, and we travelled around Thailand, India and Nepal for a year. In Chennai we met an old Indian couple, and while we were having dinner with them one night, the man looked me right in the eye and said: "I know just the right place for you two to go and live." Of course he meant Auroville. We went there, stayed for a couple of months, and loved the place. But we were not ready for it; in retrospect I can clearly see that. Still, a lot happened to us on many levels. We became vegetarian as an expression of our shift in conciousness, and felt doors were opening.

We went back to Israel, and after two years our daughter Osher Shanti was born. We felt happy and very comfortable with our way of life, though occasionally, when deeper feelings of dissatisfaction would arise and we considered moving, we would have thoughts such as: "Why try and solve a problem you don't have?" Eventually we decided to trust our feelings, and returned to India. In Rishikesh a swami suggested we stop "guru shopping", and find a place where we could do our own sadhana, somewhere that felt right for us. We thought again of Auroville.

One day I had a very strange but life confirming experience. I had done some work as a counsellor, so when an Israeli girl had been badly raped and beaten up in Rishikesh, I was asked to visit her in the hospital. I felt concerned, as I did not know how I would deal with her. That afternoon I had a nap before going to the hospital. I dreamed an old lady with a scarf around her head was climbing a flight of stairs, and in passing said: "She only needs to cry." When I visited the girl she was very detached from her emotions and I told her these same words. She wept for maybe 45 minutes, she was soaking wet from tears, and afterwards completely relieved. When I later saw a photograph of the Mother, I recognized her as the old lady in my dream. This absolutely confirmed my positive feelings about being here.

This time around in Auroville, everything initially went like clockwork. We met the right people and things flowed easily.

Talking with Aviram after 6 years

My time here has been the most difficult and the most beautiful time of my life.

When we came to Sadhana Forest there was definitely no forest here. In the area where we chose to live there was just white, bare soil, with no trees or grass.

Yorit and Aviram with daughter Osher Shanti

The rain water ran off and caused severe erosion. Our vision was to develop a reforestation project, using only volunteers, with no exchange of money. Now, five years later, the volunteers get free accommodation in keet huts, but so far we all contribute for food. I don't like doing this, but until we grow our own food, it is necessary. The community is vegan because of our love and respect for all living beings.

Things change all the time here, on a very deep level. I have had a couple of shifts of conciousness that have affected my vision of Sadhana Forest. One day a Swiss volunteer wrote in our Guest Book a lovely poem of appreciation ending with the words, "May there be forests all over the world to grow people." I realised then I was not just working with trees, but with people, and each person that passed through here was touched by the experience. This also was Sadhana Forest's purpose.

Another time an American professor said: "This is not a project, but a model." Again I had that shift of conciousness, and a realization that this could be replicated in different parts of the world. One of Auroville's International Advisory Council members, Mr. Doudou Diene, who is originally from Senegal, visited us, and was very appreciative of our vision and our approach. He was very supportive of our effort to implement the Sadhana Forest model in Senegal.

In 2007 we had 408 volunteers, far more than we ever expected. Many people come back again and we have a strong link with many of our visitors. They feel inspired by Sadhana Forest, and that basically is our vision. I remember when we started four years ago and would occasionally think, "Who will come to this far away place, as we are eight kilometres from the centre of Auroville? Who will want to work in the forest and eat vegan food?" But many people, especially young people, are looking for a conscious way of life.

One thing disturbs me very much, however; the Land Exchange policy.

It makes me sad and pessimistic about Auroville's future. I feel this is a total abandonment of the spirit of this special place; "A nail in the coffin". Auroville land is sacred land for me. I have a strong devotion to the Mother and Sri Aurobindo. When I see the land Mother has purchased for Auroville being sold, I feel extremely sad. I just hope that by Divine protection this process will not continue.

The way it is done also shocks me. There is no community consultation, no Resident's Assembly meetings on this issue. I feel this is a transition into a top-down management corporation. I was heading such a company a few years ago, and I don't want to have joined another one.

Yorit

Years ago in Israel I was trying to get admission into Art School. The students were all given a project to express our spiritual vision of our future. I was stressed that this would be my evaluation for college admission, but I tried to listen to some aspiration within me and started to work. I took a tennis ball, covered it with gold coloured pins, and carved two entrances into it. Then I made something round to contain it, like an amphitheatre. Years later, when I saw the Matrimandir, I realized what I had created.

We had a couple of beginnings with Auroville, my first exposure being in 1998. I was curious, but somehow did not make a connection with it, and we returned to Israel. Our second time was different, and I started to read the Mother and felt "as if my eyes and heart were ready."

The reality of our Newcomer period was quite difficult. We struggled to find a community, but could never find it. I realized that Israelis are very social and family orientated, and have a strong sense of hospitality with "an always open table." Our few years in the army reinforce this community feeling and we make very strong friendships. Someone in Auroville rather cynically said to me, "It will take years here before someone even offers you a glass of water." This was a very extreme reaction, but this was how the person felt.

In retrospect I can see that this is Mother's way of making one go inwards instead of always being involved in the external. Now, if someone has an understanding of Auroville, I can make a connection with them.

At first no one knew we existed, as we are five kilometres outside Auroville and at the end of a long dirt road. The Forest Group were our main friends and supporters, but now we have the Eco Film Club evenings when Aurovilians drive out to Sadhana Forest, which is used as a platform for meetings on environmental issues.

Aviram and I made the decision when we first came here to run Sadhana without using money. We realized that when money is involved your mind becomes channeled in that direction, and we wanted to be free from that way of thinking. At the beginning we used our own money, until we had nothing, but we never asked for donations. Somehow people gave, as if they realized Sadhana was not just our project, but for everyone. For example, a man built a water tower when he saw the community did not have one. Last year we received a large donation from an English man who had been here on an afternoon's tour. People feel they want to belong to Sadhana, and this is their way of expressing it. Sadhana Forest grew out of itself, we did not create it. We are only the facilitators of so much energy that revolves around Sadhana Forest. Now we know the support is there and we will never be left alone.

I feel so happy and balanced here with Aviram and my two daughters and this wonderful project. We work all the time, day and night, meeting and connecting with people and God and Mother and trees. It is a wonderfully fulfilling life.

AUDREY ... WHO CAME FROM THE USA IN 2003

I was born in California in 1933, and when I was a young girl I attended the Ohan Valley School where my best friend Radha was the daughter of Krishnamurti's secretary. I remember seeing Krishnamurti walking round the garden, and I thought of him just as an ordinary gentleman who used to keep bees and had lots of visitors. We were always told to keep quiet when they had meditation periods. One day a neighbour told me I was a very lucky girl to live near him, but I didn't know what she was talking about.

This was now war time in Europe, and my school took in lots of refugees. I remember my favourite teacher was a German, who used to talk about mountains, and an Austrian boy whom I had a crush on, and four Dutch sisters. At home our Japanese gardener suddenly disappeared when he was sent away to a camp for Japanese people after the Pearl Harbour invasion. The people I remember most fondly were our black servants, who gave us so much love and care when we were small. I could never understand, even at that young age, why some people were treated differently from others.

I later married, had three children, and lived on a ranch in the wilds of Oregon for two years. When my children were grown up I divorced my husband and began to work as an artist. It was a huge challenge for me, and I had lots of doubts and crises with selling my work, but I felt absolutely compelled to do it. I began to read Krishnamurti and other spiritual teachers, and started meditating and thinking about things on a deeper level. I took Vipassana and Zen classes and did some retreats and sort of worked out my own stuff.

On my 60th birthday I asked myself what scared me most, and what did I admire most about some women I knew. After little thought I came to the conclusion that the most scary thing I could think of would be to travel completely alone in a very different culture. I decided then and there, that is what I would do. Not quite ready to do it alone, I found a travelling companion, rented out my apartment and my studio remarkably easily, bought a rucksack, and was eager to get going, when two weeks before we were ready to leave my companion pulled out. I was devastated, and rang around everyone I knew asking if they knew anyone who would like to start a world trip. Just when I was beginning to despair a woman rang me and said; "I am going to India tomorrow; would you like to join me?" I had no idea who she was, but immediately said "Yes, yes. I would love to come with you."

After about a month of travelling around India we came to Auroville and stayed in Vérité, and I absolutely loved it. I remember my surprise at feeling so much at home. Then one day, as I was sitting in Matrimandir, I had the very clear experience of a voice saying to me: "Go, so you can be here." I knew this meant that I had to continue my trip, so I spent the next five months travelling alone in India. It was scary, exciting and fascinating.

I also wanted to challenge myself about being an artist. Was I really an artist? Is this supposed to be what I am doing? I absolutely needed to do this close self-examination; it felt like part of my soul, and I needed to look closely at it. In those five months I did a lot of drawing and painting, and began to feel that yes, it was true and real, and I was an artist.

Audrey

I returned to Auroville and rested up, but the idea of staying here never occurred to me. The very concept of the place seemed so alien and remote. It felt very colonial to me, with the ammas and servants and the white people in big houses. I only sorted these ideas out when I visited relatives in Ireland and saw the effect of colonisation on that country, and somehow compared it with India. It was all very strange and complex to me coming from the USA.

I went back to Berkeley, California, and got to know some Aurovilians who came to my drawing class. They hardly spoke of Auroville, but one day one of them asked me if I was going back there, and I had this strong feeling to come and look again.

I came back in 2003, and gradually realised that this is where I want to be. It had sort of crept up on me, but it was crystal clear that this would be my home.

Talking with Audrey after 6 years

First of all, from my perspective of course, everything is here that is in the "outside" world. It is this mysterious glue that keeps us together that I'm grateful for, and wonder at. I am no different from the way I was at home, except here any issue that I am working on is mysteriously, constantly, in my face. So I will eventually work through it, or leave. The slow guided reading I am going through of Savitri confirms my humanness while blowing my mind with the beauty of the poetry.

I am able to see where I am in this process through the illumination and resolution of the drawings and paintings I do. The facilitation of the Drawing Experiment I give teaches me how we block or open, are "ready or not!" I can't quite separate any of this – even with my family and friends in the States. I can see them much more clearly, see their importance to my process.

I am coming here in the last possible quarter of my life. Why it turned out this way, I do not know, but I don't think I am going to leave just because things may be tough at the end. I don't know; I've never been in this situation before. Auroville is beginning to organize around issues of aging and death. I want to be part of that.

LAVKAMAD ... WHO CAME FROM AGRA, INDIA, IN 2004

My parents in Agra were devotees of Krishna and my father used to read the Bhagavad Gita every evening. Karma yoga was explained to me as the highest virtue, and I see that is what I am attempting to do all these years later in Auroville. My father was the principal of a school, but I never had any ambition to be an academic, and when I was 18 I left for higher education in Germany.

My parents could not afford to send me to England, as was fashionable in those days, but as my father had a friend in Germany that is where I went. In Germany there was also the opportunity of working during the vacation, and the fees were cheaper than other countries. My father gave me enough money for my first six weeks, and after that I was completely on my own. I loved the challenge of this completely new life. I knew very little English, so I went to a language school for a month and spent most of my money right away. From my very first day in Germany people were always helpful to me. On my first morning I remember asking a man outside the station which train I should take. He took me to the ticket office, paid for my ticket, and asked the guard to tell me where to get off. This was 1958, and Indians were popular at that time, as there were very few of us – only eight at Aachen University where I studied metallurgy – and people always considered us very well behaved compared to the Arab and other foreign students.

After graduating I worked in the steel industry, and then switched to computers. In those days computers were rare in Germany and as big as a room, but it gave me an entrance to Lufthansa and the aircraft industry.

In Germany I turned against my Indian values. Only years later when I had what is called a mid-life crisis did I began to question my way of life. I came back to my roots by reading Vivekananda, Ramakrishna, and Osho ... the usual books the Westerners read to discover the East. I went on meditation courses,

Lavkamad

but never responded to any particular teachings, and was determined to find my own way.

In 2003 I retired from my job and had to face my future. Should I stay at home and look after the house and garden like most retired people did? Or should I do voluntary social or political work as the more adventurous did? I tried voluntary work, but it did not suit me at all.

Then my mother sent word that she was seriously ill, so I returned to India for three months. After one month she recovered, and I spent several weeks visiting relatives and wondering what to do with myself. Then I went to Thiruvanamalai for six weeks and met some Aurovilians, who suggested I come and visit them, which I enthusiastically did, as I was feeling very lost and aimless. There I met Karen from Lively Boutique, who introduced me to the Village Action Group, which I thought was doing wonderful work. She also told me the Industrial School was looking for an administrator with a technical background to take over the running of it, and that I might be the perfect person. The seeds were being sown for my future in Auroville. Plans had been forming in a vague way for me, as I was becoming aware that in India there are very few vocational training centres for young people as compared with Germany; and absolutely none for the poor youth. I thought it maybe a very worthwhile project to get involved with, as I had the necessary background and it would be my path of karma yoga.

I returned to Germany to wind down my life there and try to explain my decision to my family. They were understanding and supportive, as they had seen my search for a meaning in my life, and were happy that I had finally found work that would be satisfying to me. They have all been out here to visit me and we keep in good contact. This was in 2004.

Talking with Lavkamad after 4 years

I have often found things very difficult and frustrating over these last four years in Auroville. For the last 40 years I have been in business management in Germany working with planning and clear strategies. Here in Auroville people work differently – very differently. Sometimes I have found it so difficult to work in this way that I thought I could not cope, and have even thought of leaving. But always I returned to the thought that the Divine has sent me here, and this must be my path, my karma yoga that my father used to talk about. It was now necessary for me to change myself and my previous ideas, and I learn to adapt to what was here in front of me.

It is still difficult for me. When I see the lack of detailed planning, the absence of marketing strategies and the unprofessional way of working, I still get frustrated. What I find especially difficult is when people take things personally; they cannot separate the professional and personal. Yoga is not contrary to efficiency! For example, many Aurovilians only work half a day. How can we develop an economy on part-time work? Many issues are not addressed, and when things get desperate people say hopefully, "Ah, the money will come." This seems an absurd way to run an economy. This lack of professional attitude prevents many good skilled people from coming here. And we desperately need them.

The Industrial School is going well, however, and last year we had 80 students. Some of the boys can be difficult to deal with, as they come from the local villages and have little discipline, but generally most of them appreciate this marvellous opportunity that is being offered to them. Their fees cover 40% of the school's costs, and the rest we get from government grants, which are becoming more and more difficult to obtain. European money is now being directed to Africa as they have heard that "India is shining."

I have had three motorbike accidents in the last three years, and while I was recuperating I thought a lot about how Auroville will deal with its aging population. I believe there are now nearly 150 people over the age of 65 living here, and the numbers will obviously increase. I know that in the Scandinavian countries the social budgets have had to be reduced, and it will happen here and the old will suffer. Maybe we can learn from the mistakes of socialist countries.

After all, Auroville is a microcosm of the world.

DIANNA ... WHO CAME FROM ENGLAND IN 2005

As a child in a small town in the north of England I was always vaguely aware of the narrowness of the life around me, and somehow knew there must be a larger, more spacious world somewhere else. I used to love reading travel books, especially the ones where Victorian ladies rode camels across deserts wearing huge crinoline dresses. I specially identified with Mowgli from "The Jungle Book", who lived freely with animals in the forest in India.

When I was 12 my family emigrated to Canada, and we sailed across the Atlantic on the S.S. Samaria and then up the mighty St.Lawrence river. Although it was mid-April I remember the huge blocks of ice drifting by and felt their unearthly chill. I was thrilled by the vastness of the land each side of the river and understood why it was called the New World. A group of Indian students were on the boat and I was fascinated by them. I don't think I had ever seen anyone with a dark skin before. This was 1950, and foreigners were a rarity in the north of England. To me young Indian men seemed like exotic princes with their dark, elegant looks and beautiful manners. I plucked up courage to ask one of them to write something in my silly young girl's autograph book. He wrote a verse in a flowing Indian script that changed my life. In those swirls and curves a world of infinite possibilities was revealed to me. On the opposite page he wrote the translation; "May you live till the end of time, And the end of time never come. Sweet Dianna; may the heavens laugh with you in your jubilee." I never realised people could think or feel in that way, and a door to the East was opened within me. I was on my way to the New World, but I had discovered the Old. The five years in Canada were not happy .

I returned to England when I was 18 and married a Bengali law student who I romanticised as a sort of Bengali Che Guevara. It was the period when East Pakistan was throwing off the domination of West Pakistan, and our London life revolved around raising funds from the Syhleti restaurant owners around Brick

Dianna

Lane to help finance the revolution. It was an exciting, but exhausting life, and after 7 years we separated. Having lived with the warmth of Bengalis I could not bear the thought of returning to a narrow English life, and so I went with my four year old son to a kibbutz in Israel, which I vaguely imagined was a blend of Eastern and Western life. I soon discovered it was not a place to go to if you were in need of sympathy and support, especially in those raw pioneer days, so I returned to London, sadder and wiser. After a couple of years I met Norman, who has been my soul-mate ever since.

In 1976 we came to Pondicherry for me to visit the School for Perfect Eyesight in the Ashram. One afternoon we rode our bicycles the nine kilometres out to Auroville. I remember the shock of seeing the bare red earth and the skeletal Matrimandir. What on earth were these people doing here? How could these western hippies exist in this wilderness? Were they all on some crazed dream? But I did admire them, and I think I secretly wanted to be one of them. But then we went back to England, and for 28 years forgot about it.

In 2000 Norman had a double heart by-pass operation. When he recovered a little we thought of somewhere he could go to convalesce, somewhere quiet and warm, and hopefully with a spiritual aspect. For weeks we tried to think of suitable places to go, but nowhere seemed quite right. This was rather strange, as we had travelled a lot, but nowhere had made a deep impression on us. Then suddenly, out of the blue, "Auroville" popped into his head. Just like that. He was absolutely clear about going there, even in his fragile state of health, though his Indian surgeon was rather horrified by his choice of India as a place to convalesce.

We stayed at the Park Guest House in Pondicherry, and Norman visibly recovered day by day sitting on the balcony overlooking the sea. I had seen Aurovilians in Pondicherry in their shorts riding their big, dusty motor bikes and was fascinated by their healthy independence, their confidence and huge shopping bags. After a few weeks we cycled out to Auroville and I immediately loved the wide open spaces and the forests and sheer creativity of Auroville. We stayed at Centre Guest House, got friendly with Tineke, went on the three-day cycle tour – a wonderful introduction – and extended our plane ticket by six weeks.

We came back for three months each year over the next four years, but I always felt ready to go home when the holiday was over. I belonged to a philosophy school in England that was based on the Vedic teachings, so had a background to Sri Aurobindo's teachings, but somehow here in Auroville I could not make a connection. There seemed to be no particular classes, no teachings, everything seemed spread wide and loose. I could not get a grip on anything. The Ashram also seemed inaccessible, and I often felt frustrated, as if things were hidden, made difficult ... almost deliberately. I could not understand how people could live here all the time; how they could bear to see the same people every day. There seemed to be nowhere to go for a break or holiday, no network of family or friends. And all that heat and dust and bumps in the road and manic traffic...

On our fourth visit the light began to dawn for me. We spent time with committed Aurovilians instead of chatting with guests, attended classes at Savitri Bhavan, and I started Tamil classes with Shankar. Doors began to open on many levels. In retrospect, I think it was doing Matrimandir duty that finally made me feel connected. I began to feel part of Auroville, not just a spectator. It had taken a long time for me to make this connection, or for this connection to surface. When we were back in England we spent weekends with Auroville friends like Bob and Jean, Sonia, and Martin Littlewood. I seemed now to have more connection with them than my English friends, and I think this was part of the process.

When a house became available in New Creation we decided to apply for it and commit ourselves at last. Having our own house instead of living in a guest room made an enormous psychological difference. It was a physical manifestation of putting our roots down. We had become part of the Auroville community, not just casual guests.

We are in our early seventies now, and do not want to spend our remaining years in an old creation of a lifetime's habit and preferences, very comfortable though they may be. We have a wonderful sense of involvement, energy and purpose here in Auroville. And, hopefully, something to offer from our years of experience in various fields. We will now place ourselves in Mother's care for the rest of our lives.

Talking with Dianna after 4 years

As I said to someone the other day, "I feel as if I have been living under a stone for years and have now come into the light." And on another occasion "Living in Auroville I feel like a child in a sweet shop".

I always realise I am very blessed, and don't have some of the difficulties many people experience here. I have a husband who is equally involved with Auroville, we have a lovely house, and are in reasonable physical and financial health. For the first year I felt frustrated, as I could not find satisfying work and felt there was no guidance. I eventually fell on my feet when I drifted into an "Auroville Today" meeting and was asked if I would like to do an assignment. I discovered that I loved writing, especially about Auroville, and best of all, it has been my entry into its heart through meeting so many diverse and devoted people. I also work part time at Savitri Bhavan, which has opened doors to Sri Aurobindo's works and gives me direct contact with old-timers like Shraddhavan and Helmut and Vladimir.

Sometimes here I feel a great joy. This is the place I have been searching for all my life. And this is where I will end my days.

Dianna Bowler passed away on 22nd July 2012.

MANOHAR ... WHO CAME FROM ITALY IN 2005

I was born near Naples in south Italy in 1946, a very important year, as the Republic of Italy was being formed. For my parents this meant that anyone could become president of the state, and this fascinated them for years.

I was a very devoted Catholic till I was about ten, then like most people I became disillusioned with the church when I saw how the priests were not practicing what they preached.

My connection with India started with a rather strange dream I had in my early teens. In it I was a revolutionary somewhere in India, and I was in a big hall bowing down before a maharaja to be executed with a sword. I had no idea where this very clear and lasting dream came from. It felt as if it had come up from my memory cells somewhere.

My first rational connection with India was around 1964, through a very beautiful old woman who taught yoga in Naples. She was the first holy person I met, and when people years later told me about their experience of meeting with the Mother I realized that for me, at that time, she had many similar qualities. I was studying yoga asanas with her, according to the teaching of the Maharishi Mahesh Yogi of Beatles fame. Amazingly, she knew of Mother and Sri Aurobindo and talked to me about them, and gave me Satprem's "The Adventure of Conciousness," which made a deep imprint on my young mind. In this way I came to know of the Auroville project even before it was created, through xeroxed copies of the Italian "Domani", a periodical about Sri Aurobindo.

It took me years to actually get to Auroville as my busy life got in the way. I went to London in the sixties and got into flower power and psychedelics. I was always interested in music and the media and photography and worked for Krishna Lights, a workshop that made special-effect lighting, such as the Pink Floyd used. Through my work I came in contact with Bhaktivedanta Swami, who came to London to see his disciples, and got introduced into the Krishna movement. They had no temple for him to visit in London, so John Lennon lent him his beautiful house on the river near Windsor and I had an incredible week end there filming the initiations. I loved the singing and chanting but I didn't like the structure of the organization, so after a while I drifted away. I had become a vegetarian, then a macrobiotic fan, and tried absolutely everything on offer in London, and in those days that was an awful lot.

I had to go back to Italy to finish university and then do my military service, or else go to prison, but luckily I only did eight months as my son was born and I was allowed exemption. I insisted we call him Siddhartha (I had been reading Herman Hesse), poor child, and he never forgave me. I worked with record companies and traveled the world and had a great time, but of course, after a few years of high and fast living, became bored and exhausted with it. I started my own company called "Bumshiva Music" and brought new Latin American music to Italy, which diverted me for a while.

India was always present at the back of my mind, and so was this remote place called Auroville, but somehow it just sat there, simmering away on the back burner for years. Two children and a good job came along and that devoured all my energy for years. In 1982 I got myself to Nepal, which at that time was like something from the middle ages and incredibly beautiful, then went down the tourist trail to Delhi and Agra. I had been a bit frightened of going to India as people used to love telling me stories of dreadful poverty and bodies on the pavements, but of course when I got there I saw they were just people sleeping out in the open. I loved India and was charmed by the people and vowed to return as soon as possible, but of course I got caught up in my Italian family and working life again.

Then in 2002 Alitalia airlines made a special campaign to double the free flyer points for flights anywhere in the world. As I already had collected many from my travels this meant I could get a free flight anywhere in the world. I decided this was my big chance and I should grab it and finally visit Auroville. I really felt it was calling me and it was time to go. When I arrived at Chennai airport and saw the white-shirted taxi man in the middle of the crowds of Tamil people holding up a notice saying, "Manohar, Auroville", my heart jumped, and I knew was home. The incense stick and the little pictures of gods in the front of the car charmed me as we drove through the lush green countryside towards Auroville.

I arrived on February 15th, 2003, and immediately felt Auroville had captured me. The people were welcoming and Matrimandir had just been finished and the Chamber was open, and I was fascinated by it all. It was as if Auroville had given me everything, and I fell in love with it. I went on the three-day bicycle tour and everything was perfect.

I stayed in Centre Guest House and became friendly with Silvano, who used to run it with his partner Tineke. He made a great impression on me with his kindness and directness and I always saw him as the ideal Aurovilian. After one month I had one hundred per cent decided I wanted to stay in Auroville, and applied to the Entry Group for permission to stay. They told me they could give no appointments for at least a week, and I was terribly upset, as I was leaving for Italy in a few days. I thought that maybe I was acting too quickly and maybe this was a sign.

Then I went to the Matrimandir early on the morning of the day when I was to leave, and suddenly there was a violent storm with strong rain. There was nobody around because of the heavy rain, and when I came outside I was all alone, and there in the sky was a huge rainbow. I felt as if it was just for me - a "see you back soon" message from Auroville!

Manohar

Somehow I had already made the inner decision, and I went back to Italy, wound my life up there, and came back in December.

Talking with Manohar after 3 years

I have now been here three years, and every day I feel I get a new present from Auroville. I have learned to do something useful in my work as web-master of the Auroville site. I love the work, and feel as if it is "a window on the glass house" that is Auroville. When I had to return to Italy last month to renew my passport I realized how important it is in the world, as I was able to keep a good connection through the web and read News & Notes every week and Auroville Today.

I had a very strange and dramatic introduction to my work. I began on December 27th, 2004, and after a few weeks training was finally left on my own. "Don't worry; it is only a part-time job and there's not really much to do" sort of thing. After a few hours everyone in the world was hitting our website as the Tsunami had just smashed through the Tamil Nadu coast, and we got about 2,000 e-mails that day. In all the panic a guest wandered into the office asking if he could help in any way, and mentioned that he had some photos in his camera of the devastation down at Repos beach. We put them on the web and had a fantastic scoop ... on my very first day.

The Sunday Savitri study group at Savitri Bhavan gives me a lot of inspiration. One day Shraddhavan asked me if I would like to give a powerpoint presentation of Huta's paintings, and I eagerly agreed as I knew it would be a wonderful opportunity for me to deepen my experience of Savitri. We eventually decided to make the paintings into 40 minute films with music and Mother's voice, and are now about half way through the collection. I feel this is such an honour for me, to actually handle these precious paintings and be involved in such a magnificent and important work.

This is Auroville, always presenting new and marvellous opportunities if we have the open eyes and heart to see them.

I have always been a very rational sort of modern man, but I have taken the opportunity here of jumping into experiences that open up the other side of my being. I have done workshops in Reiki, non-violent communication, t'ai chi and yoga; not always easy for me, but very life enhancing, and I am discovering a potential I didn't know I had.

I sometimes feel that Auroville is the last hope of this planet. If it doesn't happen here, it will be difficult to happen anywhere else. It was nurtured by

Mother and Sri Aurobindo, and we are trying to keep up with their dream on a daily basis. It is difficult and will take time. For the last 40 years we have really just been planting trees and making shade and houses. It is a huge and magnificent project, and I am incredibly honoured to be a part of it. I feel it desperately needs protection by the Indian Government, as the commercial world is trying to get in as we make it beautiful and abundant. It is very much in India's interest to protect us, yet at the same time allow us to progress in our mistakes and controversies.

I am still in a good relationship with my wife and children back in Italy, and we have been managing to meet twice a year, which I feel is very good. Another adventure for me was living in Adventure community, which just at the time I joined was going through a difficult time. Adventure was unique among our 100-odd communities in that it attempted a way of life where people were closely involved and sharing. We took turns with the cooking once a week, shared meditation and experiences, and tried to deepen our communal life. To live so closely and share so deeply is very difficult, even alien, for westerners, and after a time we had to change our goals; now we live like the other communities, more as a neighbourhood. The spirit of the place is lost for me, but I am still there in my capsule, which I love. When I first came here I wanted to live simply and only had a large rucksack, but on my return from Italy this time I had to pay surcharge on my baggage, as now I feel I need books, tapes and the necessities of my old life that give me pleasure, and yes, comfort. You change all the time here, and you are allowed to. But I still feel proud that I can manage living in a community with only solar panels for electricity. If there is no sun there is no power and we have to use candles, which can be nice as it changes your pace and conciousness. My partner is even considering coming here, but I don't want to force her; it has to be 100% her decision.

At 61 I feel younger than I have ever felt. I feel full of curiosity for this Auroville experiment and am terribly proud to be part of it.

A YOUNG TAMIL MAN ... WHO CAME FROM PONDICHERRY

When I was in college I became fascinated by Christianity; especially the words of Christ in the New Testament. A Christian family lived nearby, and every Tuesday I would go to their house for prayers and listen to the Father reading from the Bible. I loved Christ's words, like "Ask and you shall receive; Knock and you shall enter."

My family were Hindu, and we used to go regularly to the temple to pray, but I began to feel the need for a personal God. At that time I had developed stomach problems so I prayed to God for help, and my prayers were answered. I remembered the beautiful words of faith, "If you so much as touch the hem of my garment with faith you will be cured."

One Christmas night at midnight Mass I had a turning point. My brother had come to church with me and was admiring all the beautiful flowers the church was decorated with. "What are the flowers for?' he asked me. "Just for decoration, I suppose, " I answered him. Later on he told me that flowers have another purpose for their existence, and I was very surprised. He explained that Mother had visions of the real purpose and energies of flowers. He gave me a copy of "The Sunlit Path", which to me at the time seemed rather similar to the Bible. Slowly I began to mak e contact with the Mother .

On my birthday I went to Sri Aurobindo's room and felt as if it was Christ sitting in the chair, or rather that Christ and Sri Aurobindo were the same person. The seated figure embraced me and poured out affection and love.

After coming to Mother I realized Auroville was Mother's divine dream, and I wanted to offer myself and my life to this dream. My brother and I attended all Jai Singh's classes on "Cultivating Concentration" at Savitri Bhavan, and we felt very happy . I felt Auroville was a sacred place, Mother's place, and even to spit on the ground was a sacrilege.

I realized Christ had taken me and given me to Mother.

A power is in that thou knowest not;
Thou art a vessel of the imprisoned spark.
It seeks relief from Time's envelopment,
And while thou shutst it in, the seal is pain;
Bliss is the Godhead's crown, eternal, free,
Unburdened by life's blind mystery of pain:
Pain is the signature of the Ignorance
Attesting the secret god denied by life:
Until life finds him pain can never end.
Calm is self's victory overcoming fate.
Bear; thou shalt find at last thy road to bliss.
Bliss is the secret stuff of all that lives.

Savitri

International Publications

Auroville Architecture
by Franz Fassbender

Auroville Form Style and Design
by Franz Fassbender

Landscapes and Gardens of Auroville
by Franz Fassbender

Inauguration of Auroville
by Franz Fassbender

Auroville in a Nutshell
by Tim Wrey

Death doesn't exist
The Mother on Death, Sri Aurobindo on Rebirth *Compiled*
by Franz Fassbender

Divine Love
Compiled by Franz Fassbender

Five Dream
by Sri Aurobindo

Vision
Compiled by Franz Fassbender

Passage to More than India
by Dick Batstone

The Mother on Japan
Compiled by Franz Fassbender

Children of Change: A Spiritual Pilgrimage
by Amrit (Howard Shoji Iriyama)

Memories of Auroville - told by early Aurovilians
by Janet Feran

The Journeying Years
by Dianna Bowler

Auroville Reflected
by Bindu Mohanty

Finding the Psychic Being
by Loretta Shartsis

The Teachings of Flowers
The Life and Work of the Mother of the Sri Aurobindo Ashram *by Loretta Shartsis*

The Supramental Transformation
by Loretta Shartsis

The Mother's Yoga - 1956-1973 (English & French)
Vol. 1, 1956-1967 & Vol. 2, 1968-1973
by Loretta Shartsis

Antithesis of Yoga
by Jocelyn Janaka

Bougainvilleas PROTECTION
by Narad (Richard Eggenberger), Nilisha Mehta

Crossroad The New Humanity
by Paulette Hadnagy

Die Praxis Des Integralen Yoga
By M. P. Pandit

The Way of the Sunlit Path
William Sullivan

Wildlife great and small of India's Coromandel
by Tim Wrey

A New Education With A Soul
by Marguerite Smithwhite

Featured Titles

Divine Love

The texts presented in this book are selected from the Mother and Sri Aurobindo.

"Awakened to the meaning of my heart. That to feel love and oneness is to live. And this the magic of our golden change, is all the truth I know or seek, O sage."

Sri Aurobindo, Savitri, Book XII, Epilog

A Vision by the Mother

On 28th May 1958, the Mother recounted a vision she once had of a wonderful Being of Love and Consciousness, emanated from the Supreme Origin and projected directly into the Inconscient so that the creation would gradually awaken to the Supramental Consciousness. The Mother's account of this vision was brought out a first time in November 1906, in the Revue Cosmique, a monthly review published in Paris.

A Dream – Aims and Ideals of Auroville
the Mother on Auroville

50 years of Auroville from 28.02.1968 - 28.02.2018

Today, information about Auroville is abundant. Many people try to make meaning out of Auroville – about its conception, to what direction should we grow towards, and, what are we doing here?

But what was Mother's original Dream and what was her Vision for Auroville back then?

Matrimandir Talks by the Mother

This book presents most of Mother's Matrimandir talks, including how she conceived the idea for this special concentration and meditation building in Auroville.

Memories of Auroville - Told by early Aurovilians

Memories of Auroville is a book about the very early days of Auroville based on interviews made in 1997 with Aurovilians who lived here between 1968 and 1973. The interviews presented in this book are part of a history program for newcomers that I had created with my friend, Philip Melville in 1997. The plan was to divide Auroville's history into different eras and then interview Aurovilians according to their area of knowledge. Our first section would cover the years from 1968 till 1973 when the Mother was still in her physical body.

The Way of the Sunlit Path

May The Way of the Sunlit Path be a convenient guide for activating this ancient truth as a support for a Conscious Evolution.
May it illumine the transformation offered to us in the Integral Yoga.

A Dream Takes Shape (in English, French, Hindi)

A comprehensive brochure on the international township of Auroville in, ranging from its Charter and "Why Auroville?" to the plan of the township, the central Matrimandir, the national pavilions and residences, to working groups, the economy, making visits, how to join, its relationship to the Sri Aurobindo Ashram, and its key role in the future of the world. This brochure endeavours to highlight how The Mother envisioned Auroville from its inception, some of the major achievements realised over the years, and some of the difficulties currently faced in implementing the guidelines which she gave.

Mother on Japan

I had everything to learn in Japan. For four years, from an artistic point of view, I lived from wonder to wonder. And everything in this city, in this country, from beginning to end, gives you the impression of impermanence, of the unexpected, the exceptional... ...everything in this city, in this country, from beginning to end, gives you the impression of impermanence, of the unexpected, the exceptional. You always come to things you did not expect; you want to find them again and they are lost – they have made something else which is equally charming.

Auroville Reflected

On 28 February 1968, on an impoverished plateau on the Coromandel Coast of South India, about 4,000 people from around the world gathered for a most unusual inauguration. Handfuls of soil from the countries of the world were mixed together as a symbol of human unity. Why did Indira Gandhi, the erstwhile Prime Minister of India, support this development for "a city the earth needs?" Why did UNESCO endorse this project? Why does the Dalai Lama continue to be involved in the project? What led anthropologist Margaret Mead to insist that records must be kept of its progress? Why did both historian William Irwin Thompson and United Nations representative Robert Muller note that this social experiment may be a breakthrough for humanity even as critics commented, "it is an impossible dream"?

A House For the Third Millennium
Essays on Matrimandir

Nightwatch at the Matrimandir...
A cosmic spectacle; the black expanse above, the big black crater of Matrimandir's excavation carved deep into the soil. The four pillars - two of which are completed and the other two nearing completion - are four huge ships coming together from the four corners of the earth to meet at this pro propitious spot...

Passage to More than India

This book is a voyage of discovery. In 1959 the author, Dick Batstone, a classically educated bookseller in England, with a Christian background, comes across a life of the great Indian polymath Sri Aurobindo, though a series of apparently fortuitous circumstances. A meeting in Durham, England, leads him to a determination to get to the Sri Aurobindo Ashram in Pondicherry, a former French territory south of Madras.

www.ingramcontent.com/pod-product-compliance
Lightning Source LLC
LaVergne TN
LVHW010329070526
838199LV00065B/5701